GREAT PRFIT IDEAS

BUSINESS CHECKLISTS

Great Profit Ideas is a series of cost reducing business ideas created to boost your bottom line. Use each list of ideas and actions to cut costs, improve margins, and increase sales.

GREAT PR⬤FIT IDEAS

BUSINESS CHECKLISTS

By

Donald S. Sylvester

ISBN: 978-1-71614-168-3

About The Author And This Book

Donald Sylvester has over 40 years of experience working as a controller and CFO for a number of companies located in the U.S. and Canada. Those positions all provided great learning experience and spanned several varied industries (i.e. automotive parts, book manufacturing, oil and gas supplies, parts and equipment, real estate development and hazardous waste service industries).

With this experience gained in heavy manufacturing, machining, construction (project management), importing, distribution and real estate development, Donald witnessed a number of companies improve the bottom line quickly. He thought one main reason for the continual profit improvement of these totally independent but successful business stories stemmed from one simple attribute — "Ask questions continually, be quiet and listen."

His daughter, Aura, while she was attending college classes, asked him to begin writing brief business ideas so she could learn some of the issues that face business owners every day. The one thing she insisted upon was getting to the point and creating a list of questions or ideas so the reader could understand the benefit quickly.

Donald wrote these checklists not only for Aura to learn but to be designed for businesspeople to use on their jobs. This accumulation of checklists, actions and ideas were created to simply give the reader options to choose from a number of business categories (i.e. accounts payable, production, sales, purchasing, collections, cost reductions).

As a reader, you can pick one or more and take action.

Whatever you do, remember not to ask the questions only once. Ask questions of everyone on all management levels continuously. If you try ten suggestions but only one is profitable, it will still be worth your time. Pick out those lists, questions or ideas you like. Change them to meet the needs of your company. Use them regularly and this author knows you will boost your bottom line.

Table of Contents

List Of 15 Questions To Save Money From Your Vendors

1. Am I not buying enough to get a price break?

2. Am I buying a broken quantity (split pallets, half truckloads)?

3. Am I buying at the wrong time (Grapes in December, corn in January)?

4. Is the item I insisted you make for me per my instructions over-engineered? What can I do about the material I dictated initially to you? Should we try something else, an alternative or substitute?

5. Do I need to drop my defined packaging and strap the product bare to a recycled wood pallet?

6. Can I save 35% if I buy in bulk twice per year versus placing tedious monthly shipments?

7. Did I dictate a type of material that is technically overkill and twice the price? Tell me where I am going wrong with my order. Give me some ideas to contemplate.

8. Maybe I need to let you, the vendor, redesign the item I am buying? Do you have ideas that will cut this cost? When I spoke to another competing company of yours, they told me they would redesign my product to reduce the cost. We have been doing business a long time so I feel it is only right to ask you first.

9. Maybe if I buy more items from you, the vendor, and consolidate my purchases with you, you can save me money on this item as well as the others?

10. Maybe if I pay your invoice to you, the vendor, earlier than the normal 45 to 50 days, you can offer a substantial early payment discount and save me money? (i.e. Substantial meaning greater than the normal 2%)

11. Maybe I should consider buying your company, my current vendor? I am going to think about this one by myself first.

12. Maybe I should consider hiring you and putting you on my payroll, the vendor's representative, since you know the market well and you are currently buying $50M (example) of this type of material per year and I sense you know a lot more about this product than me?

13. If I pay you, are you capable of redesigning this product that I am currently buying from you in order to lower its cost 10-15 or 20% from now going forward? Can you reconsider if I change the guarantee from 600 units to 6,000 units per year?

14. **Try putting the onus on your vendor.** There are a lot of ideas to consider when dealing with the vendor. Ask the vendor to go back to his management group and rethink what you are currently buying and come up with some proposals that will benefit both you and his firm.

15. **Talk to a new face.** Last safe suggestion: Get another bid. Go to another vendor if you do not get a good answer from your current one. One last suggestion for purchasing that always brings things into clear perspective is to get another bid. Involve another firm and get a different perspective. Go

through this same list of questions for nearly everything you buy and you will make good progress. Let the vendors come up with ideas. Your vendors are far more sharp about the items you buy from them, so allow them to help you out when you give them more business.

6 Questions To Ask Lawn Care Personnel About Their Observations When They Visit Your Property

Questions for your lawn-care vendor and its employees about observations of the buildings, grounds, specific items of trash and evidence of theft or mischief.

1. **Drainage or pipe problems**: When you are mowing, is there any area of the property that is continually wet or soggy? (possible pipe leak or water or sewer break)

2. **Break-ins, fence damage, perimeter disturbances**: When you mow or weed-eat along the wire fence-line, do you notice any places where the fence has been cut or damaged or looks like it has been forcibly opened? This may signal signs of potential break-ins or theft after hours. Thieves will cut fences and then wire them back to be used until later. Someone mowing will be able to spot this if you ask them to watch for these signs.

3. **Vagrants, suspicious vehicles outside your facilities:** While your lawn people are on the property, they are outside where most of your employees are not. For a few hours, they get to notice people, trucks and cars that seem out of place or suspicious while they are working. Ask them about this. They may have no comments and notice nothing or they tell you about issues you may wish to pursue. It does not hurt to ask these contractors what they observe and invite their comments for you if anything in the future arises. Invite them to note vehicle descriptions, license plate numbers and people's descriptions for any suspicious activities.

4. **Stolen company materials or products:** When cutting trees or shrubs, do you ever find company products or remnants in the bushes? Thieves may drop your company's product on the way out to their cars on evening and night shifts not knowing they left anything behind. This could include any type of product or company property carried out the door and put in personal cars. Have your property maintenance personnel watch for these sign of theft left outside on the property, mistakenly dropped or tossed at the last minute. Otherwise, they will walk past them, toss the items in the trash, or take them home never knowing why they were left in the company's yard.

5. **Slab or foundation problems, cracks, brick or mortar breaks:** When you are outside and trimming along the building, do you see any water running down the wall, new breaks or cracks appearing in brick-lines, or crumbling of the foundation or slab cracks along the flowerbeds and ground-line?

6. **Infestation, rodent, termite problems:** Do you see signs of squirrels, snakes or other rodents or pests left in the lawn? Do you notice any evidence along the roof lines or near entrances to buildings? These are signs that indicate the possibility you may have these creatures in the ceilings or attics of your buildings. This should also help you to analyze the pest infestation and will trigger you to schedule a pest control visit and necessary treatment.

Remember that 99% of your full-time employees come to work and never notice anything after they get out of the car and get to their workstation or desk. They have their minds on work and tasks to do for the day and never see a fence break-in or notice something stolen or lying in the yard.

They walk right past it. Items that are stolen only are noticed gone when they cannot be located. Most of your employees are oblivious to anything outside of their job duties because of the regularity of their jobs and they are numb to anything minutely different. Because of this, encourage and use the observations of your contractors and invite those to keep you informed of anything that occurs out of the ordinary in the course of their work. Remind them they cannot tell you anything that is not important; their observations and information they gather will always be welcome.

8 Reasons To Sell To Your Vendors

Most companies never think about selling to its vendors but there are hidden opportunities in tying vendors into customer relationships. Here are some to consider before you start.

1. **Vendors value your business.** Vendors being paid by you do not want to lose the business so they are more likely to listen to a sales pitch. You have bought from them, owed them money and paid your bills on a regular basis. Take advantage of this. You have shown them in the past you are good for payment so you have their attention, respect and trust. They never had to sue you for payment and they know you, plus your purchases are rising. This is 50% of the relationship that one needs in order to sell anything – a common connection.

2. **Offsetting AP and AR to pay them is easy.** Vendors that can become customers also may appreciate the ability to offset AP invoices with AR invoices so they do not have to issue checks. Accounting people and banking people do not like this but of course, they are not in sales. As long as offsets are done cleanly and both parties agree to the details, there are auditable records and it is considered by both parties as desirable, so be it.

3. **Vendor inside sales personnel own lots of clout.** The vendor's sales people have more clout than their purchasing people so remember who will win on this proposal.

4. **Target big dollar vendors who more likely to buy your products.** Look at the biggest dollar vendors. They have the most to lose by not forcing their purchasing department to consider buying from you. You have leverage here so focus on the top of the vendor list first (high dollars), then work your way down. When you tell the vendors that their competitors have these crossover possibilities and you want to do the same with them, they will start working for you.

5. **Analyze vendors as customers every quarter.** Do this analysis minimally on a quarterly basis. Your own purchasing department is changing vendors and looking for better pricing all of the time, so new names will show up every few months. Be prepared to research more selling possibilities with these new vendors on the list.

6. **A vendor may have related companies so ask upfront.** If the vendor does not purchase your product or service, do they have sister divisions or profit centers or associated companies in their firm that might? Probe this as much as possible. Many of these companies are large and some of their people do not know the sister divisions that might be right for your company. Ask your representatives to ask their bosses.

7. **A vendor may have influence on its own vendors so ask.** Some vendors are so large, they can encourage or dictate to their customers and vendors who to deal with. This is worth a try, doubtful at best, but worth asking at least once.

8. **Vendor will think twice before dumping your account.** You are far more likely to keep the current vendor longer if you are selling to him also at a good price that would be hard to find in the market.

9 Typical "What If" Questions From Your Vendors

Your purchasing personnel will most likely be able to come up with most of these types of questions for your specific vendors. Accumulate the new ones asked and add them to a FAQ section for your vendors on your website.

1. What if I tried to make a delivery and could not get through your gate because it was locked? There are no posted hours that I could see?

2. Who do I call after hours?

3. How do I get hold of anyone for your plant's receiving docks?

4. What if your employees will not sign our receiving paperwork required by my boss? Who may I speak with at your firm if this occurs before I leave?

5. What if our salesman left products for your purchasing department which asked to review them and to up to this point, we have not heard back from anyone? Is there any one person in charge of Purchasing there we can call to ask the status of your review?

6. What if we are asked for a bribe or kickback from one or more of your employees? Who do we contact? If we call anyone, we do not want to lose your account, but we do not also want to lose it because we are not participating in extortion. What do you want us to do? We would feel a lot better if you gave us a 3rd party to contact anonymously so you are notified and we remain unnamed --- would

that work? If not, please give us your policy for vendors to follow.

7. What if there is a holdup on payment of our invoices? Who do we contact?

8. What if we tried to contact the person in your AP department you gave us but there is no answer and no return call? Who do we contact then?

9. How are invoices supposed to be presented to your firm?

15 Accounts Receivable Collection Tips

Every company's list of credit customers is different but you must try different approaches. Unless your customer is paying perfectly, do not rely solely on emails and electronic generated messages because they are becoming more and more ignored. Call them which will be rare. Do something different to get their attention. Try one of these ideas.

1. **Send statements more frequently.** Fax your accounts receivable statements or email them and do it more frequently than the rest of the market. Be obviously persistent and consistent and of course, always polite.

2. **Handwrite the person's name to get attention.** Be different. Get their attention. Handwrite on the statements before forwarding them in large letters or cursive writing. You may be thinking, "No one does that!" and you would be exactly right. You want to do what no one else does. You want to get their attention.

3. **Circle items you want paid.** Circle the items you want paid and write instructions to the recipient indicating why these are late and what you expect for the vendor to do; be clear that you need these past-dues paid.

4. **Use the AP clerk's name if you know it.** You need to ask for your money first before all of their other vendors are starting to squawk. You may be inclined to just stamp the statement and send it, but you miss a unique opportunity of handwriting the person's name on the statement, something they

rarely see these days. You want attention to your request and this will do it.

5. **Fax/email first, call them on the telephone later.** When you fax or email versus calling the individuals; it is appreciated. If you fax or email an accounts payable person, they can take their time to research your past due invoices without having to stop and take your call. You are being polite by sending something that allows them time to do investigation first. This is better than calling them, catching them off guard and causing them have to answer while you are waiting on the telephone. Faxing or emailing ensures they get your message but also gives them time to research an answer so they can call back. Most will, some will not, but it is worth the first effort. This works well with commercial and mostly likely does not for individual accounts.

6. **Handwrite something pertinent, unexpected.** Handwriting gets attention because it is rarely seen anymore. Most companies are sending out computer generated statements each month if they send any out at all. When they send them, they rarely actually see the statements sent electronically. They are also virtually worthless because few pay attention to them; if sent in email, they are labeled as spam to be forever lost.

7. **Use the payers' names.** Address the AR statements to an account payable person's name if it is known. Call the company's switchboard and ask them for the AP clerk's first name if not whole

name. They are used to these inquiries and will normally provide it for you.

8. **Update names in your system.** If you have the wrong person's name on your statement, they quickly tell you so you do not continue to bother them. Take the opportunity when someone tells you that they are the wrong person to ask who the right person is and how to contact them.

9. **Ask who the current contact is (who pays you?) at every possibility.** Ask immediately and you are more likely to get an answer in order for the recipient to get you off their back. This direct communication also is taken these days as aggressive, so if you repeatedly send these out to the wrong person, they will get perturbed and tell you the right person to contact so you cease bothering them. Be polite; remember that you just want a person to contact who can pay you.

10. **Handwrite another notice.** Handwrite another note to the correct accounts payable name and send it out again. Repeat this until you get to the right person. Take advantage of the fact almost no one writes so your email or fax will be noticed most of the time. Most companies rely on dull automatically produced computer printouts which generate very little attention once received. If you take a few moments to pen the recipient's name, you will fare much better when they spot themselves on a fax machine or on an attached email from an address their receptionist gives you.

11. **Resort to the phone.** When all your faxing and emailing efforts fail, get on the telephone and call them every day until you get to speak with them. When the handwritten statements do not work and you have sent three or four unanswered emails, call your past due accounts. When they do not respond, call their switchboard and request the person's supervisor's name and ask to be transferred to that person. If necessary, as a last resort, call the buyer and ask him to help you get paid. When your firm is owed money that is growing older by the day, the last relationship you need to worry about is the one held with the buyer.

12. **Hold shipments if all else fails.** Hold this customer's remaining open shipments when the past due customer refuses to return calls. Instruct shipping personnel they are not to ship until given instructions from your collections department. Ensure this shipment is quarantined and no more work is invested in its production until you are paid.

13. **Before legal becomes involved, drag in sales.** As a last resort before legal collection efforts begin, drag in the sales person assigned to the customer to intercede. At this point your sales person who has a customer that is non-responsive and non-paying. Let your sales rep know his customer's orders are currently on hold until you are informed what is wrong and why no payment has been received. Sales people get angry when the problem grows to this point because the commission for this potential write-off of net sales will ultimately be deducted

from their bonus checks. Use this remaining available leverage. When you need to be paid, you must capture the customer's attention and use the only leverage you have. Your firm deserves an answer as to why they have not called you back or explained their non-payment. You need to be paid.

14. **Your sales rep must call on them.** Your sales representative needs to visit the customer's buyer to ask for assistance in getting the invoices paid. This is a last resort but if there is anyone else on your staff that can help, use them versus the sales person. Using the customer's purchasing agent is effective because it causes embarrassment for a position that normally should not have to be drug into a collections mess. Do it if you must to get paid. Drag everybody into the fray as early as possible before resorting to costly legal action where once it is turned over to an agency, your company no longer gets all of the monies due, but only a fraction of the original amount. Drag everyone into this collection effort before releasing this collection problem over to an agency.

15. **Your procedures timeline should trigger a collection firm.** At some point in the future (you decide the time period cutoff for your company), turn this past due amount over to a professional collection agent or lawyer. There is no reason to continue to throw money away if the customer is in financial trouble. There is also no reason to continue to try to collect from a company in trouble. The earlier you turn an account to collections, the

lower the fee and more likely it is that you will be paid.

12 Tips For Collecting Past-due AR Invoices From Customers

Try these simple tips for collecting past-due accounts receivable (AR) invoices.

1. Run a summary AR Aging every week for all credit accounts.

2. Identify all of the past due accounts (i.e. over 30, over 60, over 90, etc.).

3. Focus contact on the past-due accounts first. If this requires several days, take the time to contact each customer.

4. Call and cover all past-due customers at least once per week. Do not wait until the end of the month. You must contact them regularly until you receive payment.

5. Send them an AR Aging on the fax or attached to an email and write their own name on it. This helps to make people feel personally responsible hopefully and might provoke them to get you paid.

6. Be consistent but always be courteous and professional. Separate the AP person you are dealing with from their company's liability. It is not their fault you are not paid. Tell them you understand but will appreciate their help in any way to get past due invoices paid and resolved.

7. If you have any email program that allows you to categorize your emails (i.e. Yahoo, Outlook, G-mail), setup folders for all past-due customers. Drag all of your received and sent emails into those

folders. This will allow you to pull an email out and resend it ASAP for a follow-up. The folders will help remind you immediately who you have to contact.

8. Create a list (if you do not have one) of everyone responsible who pays you. This is all of the AP personnel that you talk to, fax to, email to.

9. When you do not have a fax or email address, write on the AR statement and mail it and print in large or noticeable legible letters on the outside "PAST DUE AR INVOICES". Few people send statements like this, especially with the AP person's name on the outside of the envelope. Do it. It works well because you stand out.

10. Address the past-due envelopes to their attention by name if known. Circle it in a color if you wish.

11. When people clear up their past-due accounts, make sure to tell them thanks.

12. Make sure to tell customers when they have credits on their account regardless of the credit's age. It will prompt them to use them and send you money. They will also be impressed you were honest to bring this to their attention.

27 Suggested Additional Listings To Make Your Company Telephone List More Helpful For All Employees

Here are some items your firm should consider adding to the company telephone list. Do not restrict copies. Make certain the receptionist, HR and your maintenance departments all are currently copied.

1. Utility name and account (if the lights/power goes off).

2. Internet provider and account (if internet access is lost).

3. Telephone company number and company account (if the land lines go down and your main switchboard is dark).

4. Telephone company number and company account (if cell phones go down).

5. Medical emergency for minor accidents ---non-life threatening (clinic name, number and company account code set up for phone-ins).

6. Medical emergency for major accidents --- heart attacks, bleeding cuts, amputations, serious falls (emergency room, hospital name, number and account code set up for telephone notifications).

7. Website problems, errors or omissions (webmaster telephone number, agency name).

8. Sales/customer service - after hours telephone number, contact name.

9. Production/warehouse – after hours, telephone, contact name.

10. General email inquiry address for distribution.

11. Medical insurance company and account number for employees. Insurance agent or broker if one is used.

12. Dental insurance company and account number for employees.

13. Short term and long term disability insurance company and account numbers for all employees.

14. Workman's Compensation carrier telephone number and account number.

15. Sheriff or county police department (hopefully never needed).

16. Sheriff or county police department (non-emergency call-ins i.e. thefts, burglaries).

17. Most common (top five or ten) freight/trucking companies used (dispatcher names and telephone numbers for tracking shipments).

18. Local truck mechanic when trucks break down on your property and need work done.

19. Local towing service telephone number.

20. Local fire department telephone number (closest to your facilities)

21. Local U.S. Post Office telephone number.

22. Name of assigned mailman and a telephone number if available.

23. Security system repair company.

24. Fire and burglary alarm system companies and service.

25. Bank telephone number and loan officer where all employee checks are cleared.

26. Local bank loan officer telephone number (where you can send vendors to cash their checks locally).

27. Federal Express, DHL, UPS, USPS telephone numbers.

Good Idea: Print the entire telephone list out and keep it at the main switchboard at all times in case your power goes out. You will use it on your cell phone to call your power company to report your outage.

24 Ideas For Employee Email Signature Videos

Your employees send hundreds or thousands of emails out every day. The place right below their signature provides an excellent place to provide a weekly link to a video featuring sales, new products, clearance events, free shipping days, two for one specials, etc. Here is a list you might consider featuring under all of those free email advertisements.

1. Show a few products or services listed in your new company catalogues.

2. Demonstrate how to operate a product.

3. Offer a recipe featuring components on sale at your store.

4. Announce free gift wrapping services with purchases over a certain threshold.

5. Show how your product is made by hand or by a craftsman in a one minute video.

6. Feature a new store location. Add a code at the end of the video for the recipient to get a discount on his or her first purchase when visiting that specific store.

7. Tell the viewers what is on sale this week and why they should go shopping or browsing.

8. What are the best store or manufacturer discount coupons offered this week?

9. Announce plating services, fabrication services, welding capabilities for a machine shop.

10. Announce a list of 20 different types of products that your cabinet shop can make that has nothing to do with cabinets. Surprise and educate your customers.

11. Announce SAT and PSAT training classes now offered on weekends at the mall or library or wherever your firm has expanded.

12. What day of the week or month can one order to get free shipping? What is included in that offering and what is not?

13. What colors are available for a featured product?

14. Offer an instructional video showing how and how not to use a product.

15. 10 easy and quick recipes for dishes using your company's food product.

16. Describe all of the benefits derived from using your company product. Explain the ease of use, savings derived and the time saved after making this purchase.

17. How difficult is it to repair, fix, return or have a product exchanged, and how is it done, step by step? Include 800 numbers, addresses to mail broken products, hours of operation and several ideas for easy fixes to try at home first before returning products.

18. Emails from doctors' offices can feature videos to discuss current flus, colds and other diseases in the area and what is being used to treat them and the symptoms.

19. Videos from restaurants, supermarkets or food and drink companies can show videos featuring five or ten-minute preparation recipes.

20. Short videos from bookstores can discuss the bestseller lists.

21. Films from veterinarian offices can discuss pet shots, grooming, signs of sickness or other issues interesting to owners of pets.

22. Videos from machine shops might show a time lapse video of a block of steel, step by step finishing process and ultimately the finished fabricated laser cut products.

23. Tax preparation offices might offer a short one or two-minute video on ten tips to save money on taxes prior to the end of the current fiscal tax year.

24. Any company might consider running a short one or two-minute video on how to save money when a consumer considers buying (fill in any product name).

When Sales Are Failing, Try This List
Of 32 Marketing Actions

Try one or several of these ideas when your company sales are lagging behind your forecast.

1. Create brief but effective company literature for mailing to potential customers. Keep it concise, colorful, eye-catching. Always tell the buyer what to do. State a specific call to action (Call Us Today For Your Free Quote 1-800-999-9999!).

2. Fax black and white versions of your company literature or specials to potential customers. Keep the fax copies that fail on the first try and redial them later. Some office machines may be busy.

3. Leave flyers in your lobby every day and encourage all visitors to take them.

4. Hang flyers in racks along the walls of your offices, warehouse, shipping as well as sales departments so that during tours they are easily found and distributed.

5. Give flyers to all of your company drivers to offer and to leave with customers at drop off points.

6. Teach all of your employees what the company special is for the week or month. Post it clearly on the announcement board and test employees randomly about the week's special so they may clearly repeat it to potential buyers.

7. Give flyers to your quality control personnel, who many times will meet with their customers' counterparts.

8. Give flyers to your shipping department to be sent with freight shipments. Include them with the packing lists.

9. Send flyers with your company invoices. You have already paid for the stamp so send them free in the same envelope.

10. Send flyers along with your payments. Ensure not to exceed the weight of one stamp in order not to incur additional postage costs.

11. Give away low cost items with high perceived value by your customers (i.e. free tie with shirt purchase, free coffee with doughnut purchase, free whip cream with purchase of two pies, free metal plating with machining order, free maps and city nightlife coupons with a weekend stay hotel package).

12. Identify several of your major customers' SIC codes (Standard Industrial Classification codes) and buy lists of companies listed under those codes. You may be more likely to sell to them since you are already in the market.

13. Place samples of your products to give to your customers everywhere in your plant, office, warehouse, distribution center, kiosk (all company facilities, rented or owned or shared).

14. Give company literature to purchasing personnel to attempt to sell to vendors. Consider trading

products or services with vendors along these lines. Do your vendors even know what you sell? Tell them so they tell others. Remember to do the same when asked of you.

15. For each employee, ask them to tell their contacts that the company is featuring specials. Sometimes simply asking triggers third and fourth party interest. You do not know who you will contact through second and third conversations.

16. Give something away free on all mailers to provoke interest. Give away tips, advice, a price reduction, an added bonus that is normally sold and may be valued by the buyer. Give away 10 great and helpful tips to the buyer and then offer another 10 when he calls and signs up free of charge. Make the items you give valuable to your targeted market. Tell him information he most likely will not know.

17. Sell to your neighbors and others in your city, neighborhood or industrial park. Create a listing of all of your neighbors and pass it out free to them. Describe briefly what each does and include telephone numbers. Since they are the cheapest customers to work for, give them a neighborhood discount that no other company receives. Give them expedited service since they are across the street or just down your road nearby.

18. Go through your current accumulated customer list and approach any customer that has not returned in two years or more. Buyers change, companies change and any previous sour relationship probably

does not exist now except in your own mind. Companies never stay the same so call them if you have not heard from them for a period of time. Try assigning them to a new friendly and engaging sales person. He or she can tell them your company has grown, your costs are now even more competitive and you have gained great experience over this time. Send them samples and court them as if nothing unpleasant ever occurred.

19. What is the actual out of pocket costs of your quote? Teach sales personnel and those people who quote for you how to determine how to deduct the fixed portion of your quoted overhead. Fixed overhead is property taxes (paid once per year), rents, fixed personnel (QC, maintenance, receiving, shipping, production personnel). Determine how much your quoted costs drop in order to negotiate better pricing and win bids. You cannot do this forever but it will help you to win work that at least will not be an immediate cash drain.

20. Follow up on outstanding quotes. Know how low you can drop your price to win work and save your customer money. Call before the determination is made in order to attempt to sway the buyer to your bid. If you are told you are high, ask by how much. Train your personnel as to what to quote with the next number in order to win bids.

21. Bid first jobs with new customers low enough to win the order. Do what you can to win the first bid to show the customer what your firm can do. Do not worry about initial losses or poor margins. You

can increase your efficiency or, improve your methods of production later. Once he is happy, he will be much more likely to allow you more margin in future bids. Prove yourself first. If you do not get the first bid, all of your marketing efforts are worthless.

22. With your bids, offer unique approaches to the buyer along with his original request. Give him alternatives he may not have considered. Educate your buyer since he buys lots of products and services but is not an expert for any. Give him prices with and without freight, low and high volumes or prices coupled with other purchases that can give him discounts.

23. When bidding to customers, give the buyer a bid as he requested and also hand him a bid that drops the price for his request if he also buys other services or products that maybe his current vendor does not provide. This will put pressure on his current vendor and cause him to rethink his current relationship.

24. Use brightly colored labels on all of your outgoing mail to advertise current company specials. Feature your call in free 800 number and include a clear call to action (Call Us Today!) and offer something of value for free when the recipient calls for a quote.

25. Add advertising to all your employees' outgoing emails. Feature the company specials or discuss new products or services. If warranted, add a link for a quick 30 second video about a new product or

service you now offer or improvements made to existing products. Feature all of the benefits or uses of your product and place it under every employee's signature to be seen by those contacted outside the company.

26. Create a one page company summary or resume. Pack as many things as you can into one letter size page. Include telephone, fax, emails, websites, product listings, locations, services or products provided, a varied list of accomplishments unique in the industry, possibly a listing of current customers, key personnel, selected pictures or representative icons, ISO status, certifications necessary, hours of operation.

27. Create a page of all of your product lines or services. Make it clear and concise limiting it to one page. No one wants long lengthy brochures any more. Keep it to one page. If they want more, pull out your catalog.

28. Prepare a list of tips or advice for your customer on how to choose a company like yours. Give him lots of details how to save money and give this list out freely. Make sure he learns something from this listing so he has the perception this company seems to be the most knowledgeable.

29. Describe what all of the uses are for your product. What can be cleaned with your detergent or soap or cleaning fluid? What recipes can be made with your gravy mixture? What can be prepared with your flavoring? What can be made from your

special grade of stainless steel and what industries buy this grade?

30. Review your business cards. Can one tell what you sell? If the reader does not understand what your firm offers, sells, makes or services, the writer has failed and confused the buyer. Be clear how you can bring benefits to the buyer. Tell him what you can do for him specifically.

31. Feature pictures of your good-looking salespeople on their business cards and on your website. Many times they will leave their card and it might not be thrown away if it gets the buyers' attention.

32. Always remember to sell the benefits and not the boring product. People buy the ½ inch hole and not the drill. They buy the trimmer waist and not the weight reduction bar. They buy the clean smell of the automobile after it has been washed and vacuumed. They buy a more attractive appearance than just a fifteen minute haircut.

18 Ideas For $20 Stamp Pad Advertising

When your firm is low on advertising money but needs sales, buy a cheap stamp and ink pad and advertise on all of your envelopes going out the door, invoices sent to customers, packing lists accompanying products and any other piece of paper you think your customer will see. Here is a list of stamp pad messages you might consider. Use a bright color for your specific announcement.

1. New products or services (We Do Lawns And Sprinklers!, Double Fudge Chocolate Coming!, Low Cost Pool Maintenance Plans Available!, We Clean Your Bricks While You Work!, Free Car Drop Off Services!, Ask About Free Breadsticks!, Tune-Up While You Wait!)

2. New product features (free luggage rack with car purchase, five years of free oil changes on any car purchases made during January, etc.)

3. Our warranty programs extended from one year to two years with purchase of any new car currently on our lot.

4. New product colors, features or size options (buy stamp pad ink featuring the color being announced).

5. Announce new store hours or customer service switchboard hours.

6. New website upgrade (make sure your website address is part of the stamp or printed on your envelopes).

7. New store locations (Announcing our new store in Livingston).

8. Something free given with minimum purchase amount (feature FREE in large letters and the call to action).

9. Ask a question (answered when they call your 800 number).

10. Announce a contest and the dollars awarded (contest featuring best photo using your product, random selection every 30 days).

11. Announce your anniversary date (our 50th year).

12. Announce a new salesperson (give their name and how to contact them to place an order).

13. Announce hiring programs for machinists.

14. Announce free freight on orders over a dollar threshold.

15. Announce tax free weekends.

16. Announce 24 hour delivery.

17. Announce one day turnaround on any order over $100

18. Tell customers what they did not know about your capabilities.

40 Ideas For "Yes" Advertising Messages Conveying Information To Your Customers

Try a "Yes" campaign which emphasizes positive statements about your firm the customer may not know and be glad to learn about it.

Here is a list of "Yes" statements to peruse. "Yes" campaign labels to advertise all of your features and capabilities such as these.

1. Yes, we take calls 24 hours a day.

2. Yes, we have our own service department.

3. Yes, we galvanize almost anything.

4. Yes, we can take care of that.

5. Yes, we can solve your plumbing problem.

6. Yes, we love to match and exceed competitor coupons.

7. Yes, we export....every day.

8. Yes, we deliver overnight....if that is what you want.

9. Yes, we can ship rail.

10. Yes, we have delivered to South America, Asia and Europe.

11. Yes, we have our own trucks.

12. Yes, we pick up and deliver. Just tell us directions.

13. Yes, we take the old refrigerator away, if you ask.

14. Yes, we clean\up your yard before we leave.

15. Yes, we have a mark- down bin. Check it out.

16. Yes, we have great volume discounts. Just ask.

17. Yes, we do windows….both sides.

18. Yes, we sell 'adult' cakes. Just ask, when the kids aren't around.

19. Yes, we help you get bigger tax refunds.

20. Yes, we help you pass the CPA test….if you study.

21. Yes, we do tutoring in your home.

22. Yes, we will be there when you tell us.

23. Yes, we assemble any toy you buy, if you ask.

24. Yes, we repair everything we sell.

25. Yes, we take credit cards.

26. Yes, we issue refunds without a hassle.

27. Yes, we have extended store hours now.

28. Yes, we have gift ideas for you!

29. Yes, we still have your layaway!

30. Yes, you can leave your kids in our playroom while you shop.

31. Yes, we provide escorts to the parking lot for your convenience. Just ask your cashier.

32. Yes, we cash federal and state tax return checks.

33. Yes, we ship your 'adult' products in plain unmarked packaging.

34. Yes, we will take returns back for 30 days.

35. Yes, we will take our sister stores' returns.

36. Yes, we are open until 12 midnight. Yawn!

37. Yes, we are open 24 hours a day.

38. Yes, we giftwrap for free.

39. Yes, we will be open Christmas Eve (until 8 pm).

40. Yes, we have layaway.

25 Simple Cost Reductions You Can Start Today That Will Boost Your Bottom Line

All companies run into periods of lower sales in which to maintain profitability your employees must do different things and address cost problems. Try one or more of these ideas to cut costs today.

1. **AC/Heating waste:** Assign specific people to turn off or drastically turn down AC and heating equipment at night to cut down on energy usage, especially in offices and portions of your company's buildings that are uninhabited large time periods of the day.

2. **Energy usage:** Assign someone or more to turn off all space heaters, overhead lights and other equipment, small and large in unused offices or warehouses at night.

3. **Sell your empty truck miles:** Go to the internet and fill your empty returning trucks with paid freight. Haul partial shipments (LTL or less than a load). You will find freight back haul and LTL internet boards that advertise loads every day wanting empty trucks to take small or LTL paid loads. Do not allow your trucks to return to your facility with something helping to pay on its way back home. Consider giving your drivers an incentive for helping to procure any backhaul. You want them on the telephone every day demanding backhauls before they return to your facility to reload for the next shipment.

4. **Off brand office supplies:** Make a second person question and review the office supplies that are bought. Insist on buying very few name brand items. Demand off brand items be purchased. Make your office supplies vendor give you a list of their cheaper substitute items to buy. Limit the number or types of items that are being purchased. Make supervisors approve of their employees' purchases. You do not want 27 colors of highlighters, expensive legal pads, etc.

5. **Calculate your net profit before accepting purchase orders:** Make your estimating department declare what your company will earn BEFORE accepting customer purchase orders. Declare what your estimated net profit % will be before accepting and signing off on new customer sales orders. Make your sales manager sign off on estimates prior to accepting customer orders.

6. **Check all new incoming sales orders for any changes to terms:** Every incoming sales order should be checked to make sure the pricing is the same as the quote your firm gave, freight and taxes are unchanged, due dates are acceptable and the customer's payment terms are acceptable and not different from that quoted. If there any problems, do not accept the purchase order and call the customer's buyer to make the necessary correction. Many companies send their purchase orders via email and they are never reviewed to find discrepancies with the original quotes.

7. **Clean up orders before shipment:** Do not allow any incoming orders to be taken without written pricing covering freight and taxes. Avoid arguments with customers by doing the proper job upfront at the order desk. If necessary, do a final check within shipping prior to the release of outgoing orders in order to make sure everything is in place for final billings to the customer (over or under shipments approved, delivery date confirmed, delivery address acknowledged, purchase order received and correct from customer, pricing approved, freight terms correct, sales taxes declared and at correct rate).

8. **Ask vendors for revised quotes:** On a potentially large bid opportunity, you want your best quote in front of a potential customer. Before turning in your bid, call your outside vendor to get their best price for this unique large opportunity. Tell the vendor his lower price will be reserved just for this bid but you need them to get their pencil out so the overall opportunity is not lost.

9. **Quotes unfinished:** Determine how long a quote should take to respond to a customer. Set the turnaround time in stone and measure the department's performance. The estimating department does not leave until all quotes are turned in to ensure quick response to new potential customers. Report quotes unfinished and their age every day.

10. **Bill shipments quickly:** Determine how much time should lapse between the time a shipment goes

to a customer and when that invoice is billed to the customer (i.e. internet billing, invoice cut and mailed, invoice cut, scanned and emailed to the customer). Report the dollar value of all shipments not billed, reasons for each billing delay and their ages every day.

11. **Employee assignments at day-end:** Assign employees a checklist of things to do before leaving for the day. Pick up trash, clean work area, gather up supplies that are to be used again or are recyclable, stack material neatly in the plant, put tools back in order, ensure all parts have been reported to QC, all material used is reported to inventory, turn in material usage sheets and report any machinery problems to the production supervisor before leaving.

12. **Assign minimum daily sales calls:** Assign a minimum number of sales calls to be made every day by each sales person to be done before they leave for the day. Ask them what they are doing that someone else could do so they can sell. Ask them every day and teach those around sales to continue this tradition.

13. **Daily brochures and handouts:** Have your truck drivers give all customers company brochures announcing new products, new services or new features that our company now offers. Drop them off on all new delivery routes or stops. Ask your quality control department to hand these out to visiting customers during audits. Ask your production personnel to have them available in the

plant or in your warehouses to pass out to visitors. Include all departments in selling.

14. **New customer mailers:** For every new customer set up during the day, research the names and addresses of all associated sister divisions and branches. Mail brochures offering corporate discounts to those locations and buyers. Have the sales person tell the new buyer he can most likely get a further discount from your company if he can get his company's other buyers to also place orders with your company.

15. **Mail targeted advertisements every day:** Make sure to mail 20, 30 or 100 new advertisements, brochures, discount coupons or whatever mail that will gain new customers or will entice other potential customers to call for a quote. You pick the number to target every day but do it consistently no matter what. Make it a daily habit. Make sure your mailing inserts and brochures are up to date, relevant to the market, interesting to the potential reader and finally provoking enough to cause the recipient to call your firm. Place stickers on the outside of your mailers to invite them to read the inserts and make it easy to call you anytime.

16. **Ask new callers how they heard about the company.** Find out why customers called your company. Write down the reason stated by new callers when they call looking for a quote. Was it from a conversation they had with someone? Was it from literature from our company received in the mail? Was it from a sales call made by our sales

person? Was it from a referral by our current customers or vendors? If there is more than one answer, identify the main reason they called. We need to acknowledge referrals and reward them. No matter what, find out what causes your company to obtain new customers.

17. **Ask sales people what keeps them from selling:** Poll the sales people as to why they cannot sell and do it every day. What stops them? What procedure do we have that stands in the way of getting new sales orders? What keeps them from finalizing and receiving a customer purchase order? What procedure or department does not work or hinders that sales person from getting new business? Has anything happened in the market that dictates that our company must change to respond to the market? Anything that has happened that will change our ability to get new orders or get orders out the door?

18. **Ask receiving people about returns:** Find out what products are being returned every day. What is wrong with our products that the customer determined they were not worth the cost or did not work as portrayed by our sales people? Ask the receiving people every day what has come back and the reasons for the return. (i.e. wrong color, bad finish, incorrect parts shipped, parts do not work, ruined product shipped to customer, delivery was late, product failed under the customer's QC plan, etc.)

19. **Ask employees who holds them up every day:** Ask every day where the employees see the largest

waste in your company. Ask about wasted products, effort or time performing daily tasks or the normal workload. Ask what can be trimmed, reduced, cut and what actions currently being performed do not work. Ask what department seems to be running without direction, which company departments are constantly behind, holding up workflow, stopping billings, slowing shipping, etc. Ask the question because every employee will most likely have answers that are not yet known.

20. **Ask employees what about the company can be improved:** Pass out slips to all employees to find out what they think needs to be improved within the company. Invite them to cover anything they want but get their ideas back at the end of the first day. Let them talk about anything. They will fill your ears with plenty of items to work on challenging the company, some of which you were unaware.

21. **Add approval levels for spending:** If you need to cut your costs, assign a senior level of manager to approve spending in the purchasing department before monies are committed. Give him instructions for now that he is to stop any discretionary spending that does not support sales or production in some direct manner. His instructions should be to buy only critical items in order for sales and work flow to continue. If he has problems with understanding this, he too may be part of your company's overall cost problem.

22. **Most overtime worked:** Find out who worked the most overtime yesterday and why. What was

another alternative that was not considered before having a man work 16 hours in production? Who was working and why? How many hours did they work? Was there any possibility that they could have gone home on normal time and finished the job the next day? Who determined for the employees to work 16 hours? Did the customer pay for this? Did anyone ask the customer this question?

23. **How many failures in quality control today:** Ask how many product failures were detected during the day and request the reasons. Any particular operators, shift, set of machines, specific difficult products? Any trends noted?

24. **How many customers were angry today?** Ask the receptionist about any angry customers? Ask if there were any and how they were handled. Does that receptionist know for a fact that the customer was handled with courtesy and got his question answered or his problem solved? If the receptionist does not know, follow this up to find out the procedure and how it worked within the sales department. If it did not work for the customer positively, assign the sales department to contact that customer to ensure he is satisfied with everything that happened subsequently to his order.

25. **Review your list of offsite records and destroy those records outside the legal limit.** If you keep company records offsite, print a complete listing of the boxes they hold and get rid of those outside the legal limit. Boxes containing tax records need only

be retained for a set number of years. Customer purchase orders and contracts are to be retained for a set number of years. Find out what these legal limits are and destroy all boxes outside those parameters. This will immediately cut your storage bill at this outside facility.

Try This List of 66 Ideas To Increase Your Company Profits

Here is a list of ideas to try, actions to take and changes to make in your organization all designed to boost your bottom line.

1. **Pay incentives quickly**: Reduce the time to pay incentives after your salespeople bring you a new purchase order. (i.e. pay them the following week, not the end of the month). Put the meat on the dog's nose so he can see it, not on the other side the road.

2. **Maximize selling time**:   Reassign tasks to eliminate the time salespeople are NOT in front of or talking to potential customers. Your aim is to double their time in front of or talking on the phone to potential or current customers. Do you want to pay them to sit and keypunch orders, answer junk email or got get the first purchase order from a new customer?

3. **Issue complete POs**: Issue all purchase orders with firm pricing covering all freight, tax responsibilities and possible late charges. Cover all possible charges upfront. Leave no questions unanswered when you issue a purchase order.

4. **Bill fast**: Bill all shipments within one day (one hour, four hours, etc.) or less. You select the ideal time limit for your type of company. Many of your

customers' AP (accounts payable) clerks start the payment clock when they receive the invoice (email or mail) and not from the shipment date (actual transfer of title) so speed up the billing process regardless of where you are starting.

5. **Find out reasons for late payments**: Make polite collections calls every day for everyone with late invoices. Watch for and listen to reasons why customers are late. Is it wrong pricing, bad products, late deliveries, waiting on your salesperson to respond to their complaint? Make sure the payment is late due to slow cash flow and not something your firm has done wrong. Eliminate all of their reasons not to pay that you can ASAP.

6. **Who owes money?** Run the AR Aging every day and pay attention to late customers. Be polite but be diligent. Eliminate all reasons which held up payment. Make collections every day politely, but persistently.

7. **Is the PO the same as what you bid?** Review all new incoming customer purchase orders for term problems or discrepancies such as price, delivery times, freight, taxes and all other requirements. If there are any disagreements, work them out before accepting new purchase orders (commitments). Never blindly accept customer orders.

8. **Take cash**: Always sell for cash. It is irrelevant how much they already owe you OR how much you wrote off due to them. Swallow your pride and turn your inventory back into cash.

9. **Cut the lights off**: Hire an electrician to install lights that automatically turn off and thermostats that automatically shut AC or heat down after hours. Go ahead and do it and stop considering it.

10. **Fast quote turnaround**: Submit quotes to potential customers within 24 hours (you pick the cutoff). If you are late with bids, potential customers will think you most likely will be late with the product or service delivery.

11. **Learn from lost bids**: When you lose a bid, find out why. Ask the dollar difference, equipment or design advantage you didn't have in your bid. Find out and understand the bid approach that beat your proposal. You want to know all of the reasons why you were not awarded this bid so you can change your approach, tighten your belt or understand you are not qualified in this market. Ask yourself, "Is it a lack of capital, equipment or do we have a lack of good sharp bidders?"

12. **Rebid until rewarded**: When you lose a bid, make sure to bid to this company and this buyer again. Each time they are more likely to lean toward your bid because of your tenacity and also because

they need bidders. They know if they do not give you something at some future date, you will finally stop and not waste your time bidding.

13. **More sales with existing customers**: When you set up a new customer, find out all of the names, addresses, buyers names, telephone numbers of all of the related sister divisions upfront. These are the reasons you will offer corporate discounts and give your first buyer a further cost reduction when he/she helps you to sell to his sister divisions.

14. **Pay for broadening markets**. Pay incentives for new customers regardless of the margins. Your firm needs new customers and a broader, more diverse customer base. This small new customer may grow to be the company's largest in the future. You will not know unless you obtain their business and ask about other possibilities where you can make inroads. You are paying for opportunities, not today's margins.

15. **Pay for more GP $**. Pay an incentive when your sales representatives raise the average gross profit margin of their assigned customers. Show them the weighted average margins of each customer and tell them they will financially benefit when those numbers rise.

16. **How many calls today**? Establish a minimum number of new potential customers to call or visit

every day or week before anyone goes home. Once you start this and they begin making more money, the requirement becomes irrelevant for your successful reps.

17. **Announce the targeted customer list**: Put the list of customers your company would like to do business with on the wall in clear view for all employees to see. Ask your employees who knows anyone who works there. Any leads and connections may be worth small bonuses or employee gifts. Involve everyone in securing new business.

18. **Ask for potential customers**: Ask your employees to submit companies where your firm should solicit business. Get them involved in the process and reward them when those efforts turn into new orders. You will also be glad to pay visiting vendors for their suggestions that payoff. For those individuals, you will send their checks to their house.

19. **Correct product delivery due dates**. Watch and eliminate 'late' shipments. Change due dates accordingly when customers are late delivering their part of the agreement. Discuss this immediately and get them to acknowledge the date change.

20. **Measure lousy service**. Ask the receptionist which salespeople will not or hesitate to speak with

customers. Ask which sales personnel own the most complaints by their assigned buyers/ companies.

21. **Angry customers**? Ask the receptionist every day which customers are upset, angry or perturbed. Request that he or she keep a log of customer complaints after writing down contact names, customer names, telephone numbers and email addresses. Someone must return those calls and apologize for the delay before leaving the day the complaint was made. Do not let an angry customer go to sleep with this irritating him. Have someone call and genuinely apologize the same day.

22. **Lost sales reasons**. Ask your salespeople when and why they have to say "no" to customers. Ask them what causes them to lose sales, disappoint or fail customers? If they are losing sales incentives, they will be glad to tell you why. Is it production, purchasing, lousy QC inspections, missed shipment dates, poor quality shipments or high prices that do not match the benefit purchased?

23. **Pay for problem identification**. When you offer incentives to your production personnel for increased production, offer to pay them also for their best ideas on why production failed. Since they were cheated out of potential bonuses, they will tell you, quickly.

24. **What are the most returned products?** In addition to asking quality control, ask your receiving personnel which of your products fail the most. Since they see the trucks bringing those failed parts back into the receiving dock to be reworked or replaced, they recognize these failures far too often. They are most likely your experts on company failures and the reasons why those products fail.

25. **Watch chargebacks.** Ask the billings clerks to tell you which customers debit back (charge back) your company the most? The billings person cannot approve debits so when they are noted deducted on incoming payment receipts. Who in sales approves the credit memos to recognize these deductions? Who authorizes a subsequent internal credit to adjust AR? If there is not a summary report issued to a number of eyes, there should be on a regular basis.

26. **Watch billing errors.** Ask the billings clerks to report and classify all credits issued during the day, week or month to customers and rank them dollar-wise high to low. Who authorizes those credits and what is the dollar cutoff before a higher authority must approve? How about a minimum each and a total minimum for analysis?

27. **Classify billing errors by type.** Ask the billings clerk to summarize the month's credit memos issued sorted by cause of problem. (i.e. wrong

price, wrong quantity, defective parts discovered by the customer, billed to the wrong company, billed with freight and tax errors, billed incorrect format, mailed versus internet, mailed versus emailed). Once analyzed, call in department managers to review which processes are failing for correction. Maybe some specific 'irritating', 'costly' or 'difficult' customers need to be fired (by raising prices).

28. **How many late orders?**   Monitor the total amount of late order $ and as a % of total outstanding orders. Are the due dates updated? Are the due dates adjusted when the customer is at fault causing the shipment delay?

29. **Cycle count monitoring**:   Watch and monitor inventory cycle count charges per month (gains netted against losses).   Are they rising, falling or staying about the same? Are cycle counts made from the floor to the books and the books back to the floor?

30. **Free ads**:   Advertise freely on the front of your mail (use stamp pads, labels, stickers announcing new products or services). It already has a stamp on it so why not use the free freight to convey a message to all of your customers and vendors?

31. **Sell excess stock**.   Drag your excess inventory out to remind all to sell it. Publish a list, put it on your

website, drop the price further each month, sell it back or trade it with your vendor, pay incentives to move it and stick with a rigid plan for cleaning out stock on a regular basis. Set up an automatic procedure that brings unsold or unpicked stock to this clearing area for removal and markdown.

32. **Ask for savings**: Ask vendors how to save money when you buy from them. Ask for off brands, specials, overstock sales, substitutes, etc. Tell them you don't want to go elsewhere for now and know they want to help.

33. **Your vendors have answers**: Ask your office supplies vendor to give you a highest to lowest list of items bought, suggested substitute products and volume price reductions if you stick with his firm. Make it his responsibility to make sure you realize a savings during the next 12 months.

34. **Alternate buyers**: Change out or alternate buyers for vendors to submit bids. If they cannot rely on submitting their bid to the same known quantity, they may be reluctant to mark it up too much. Tell them their bids cannot be changed. You are receiving one bid alone and it be received by a different buyer than they have known in the past. You must instruct buyers NOT to discuss these bidding procedures among themselves in order to get further savings from the vendors.

35. **AP and Sales are neighbors**: Sell to your vendors. Sit AP personnel next to the Sales department. Make each group look at the other's list of companies (customers and vendors) and look for opportunities. Try to buy from your customers. Try to sell to your vendors. Sell to vendors with whom the company has leverage. Customers will be dumbfounded when you begin buying from them and less likely to dump you for another vendor.

36. **Show what you make**: Post photos of your products everywhere; lobbies, hallways, company printed material, envelopes, stationary, packaging, etc. Photos will teach buyers what you have to offer. That is why storefronts show pictures so that drivers can spot them while driving by.

37. **Ask for problems:** Pay a weekly bonus to employees to identify the biggest production pitfall, delay, problem, roadblock, etc. When you pay them, they become geniuses and will identify any hitch in the production schedule that occurs. You want this to happen and you want to tell all of the employees you are willing to reward their valuable input. Announce the winners and show the money going into their happy hands.

38. **Reasons for sales**: Ask customers why they bought your product. You may be surprised. Do not taint the answers. Keep the question simple and let them respond. You will use all of the unknown

reasons in your next advertisements to provoke new sales.

39. **Teach courtesy**: Teach your shipping personnel how to treat customers. Your customers may be sending trucks to your facility to pick up items. They don't need to be slighted, ignored or treated badly by your shipping staff.

40. **Raise prices on bottom GP performers**: Line up all customers by profitability and make money by raising prices on all of those with overall negative gross profit margins. Raise prices for all those jobs or products that cause this negative GP results. If those customers leave, you will make money. If they accept price increases and decide to stay, you make money. You cannot lose except by delaying your decision to do this.

41. **AC/Heating waste:** Assign specific people to turn off or drastically turn down AC and heating equipment at night to cut down on energy usage, especially in offices and portions of your company's buildings that are uninhabited large time periods of the day.

42. **Energy usage**: Assign someone or more to turn off all space heaters, overhead lights and other equipment, small and large in unused offices or warehouses at night.

43. Sell your empty truck miles: Go to the internet and fill your empty returning trucks with paid freight. Haul partial shipments (LTL or less than a load). You will find freight back haul and LTL internet boards that advertise loads every day wanting empty trucks to take small or LTL paid loads. Do not allow your trucks to return to your facility with something helping to pay on its way back home. Consider giving your drivers an incentive for helping to procure any backhaul. You want them on the telephone every day demanding backhauls before they return to your facility to reload for the next shipment.

44. Off brand office supplies: Make a second person question and review the office supplies that are bought. Insist on buying very few name brand items. Demand off brand items be purchased. Make your office supplies vendor give you a list of their cheaper substitute items to buy. Limit the number or types of items that are being purchased. Make supervisors approve of their employees' purchases. You do not 27 colors of highlighters, expensive legal pads, etc.

45. Calculate your net profit before accepting purchase orders: Make your estimating department declare what your company will earn BEFORE accepting customer purchase orders. Declare what your estimated net profit % will be before accepting and signing off on new customer sales orders. Make your sales manager sign off on estimates prior to accepting customer orders. He or she would not do this with their own money at home so they should not do it with the company funds.

46. **Check all new incoming sales orders for any changes to terms:** Every incoming sales order should be checked to make sure the pricing is the same as the quote your firm gave, freight and taxes are unchanged, due dates are acceptable and the customer's payment terms are acceptable and not different from that quoted. If there any problems, do not accept the purchase order and call the customer's buyer to make the necessary correction. Many companies send their purchase orders via email and they are never reviewed to find discrepancies with the original quotes.

47. **Clean up orders before shipment:** Do not allow any incoming orders to be taken without written pricing covering freight and taxes. Avoid arguments with customers by doing the proper job upfront at the order desk. If necessary, do a final check within shipping prior to the release of outgoing orders in order to make sure everything is in place for final billings to the customer (over or under shipments approved, delivery date confirmed, delivery address acknowledged, purchase order received and correct from customer, pricing approved, freight terms correct, sales taxes declared and at correct rate).

48. **Ask vendors for revised quotes**: On a potentially large bid opportunity, you want your best quote in front of a potential customer. Before turning in your bid, call your outside vendor to get their best price for this unique large opportunity. Tell the vendor his lower price will be reserved just for this bid but you need them to get their pencil out so the overall opportunity is not lost.

49. **Quotes unfinished:** Determine how long a quote should take to respond to a customer. Set the turnaround time in stone and require the department to measure its performance. The estimating department does not leave until all quotes are turned in to ensure quick response to new potential customers. Report quotes unfinished and their age every day.

50. **Bill shipments quickly**: Determine how much time should lapse between the time a shipment goes to a customer and when that invoice is billed to the customer (i.e. internet billing, invoice cut and mailed, invoice cut, scanned and emailed to the customer). Report the dollar value of all shipments not billed, reasons for each billing delay and their ages every day. Find out the guilty party who is holding up invoicing.

51. **Employee assignments at day-end**: Assign employees a checklist of things to do before leaving for the day. Pick up trash, clean work area, gather

up supplies that are to be used again or are recyclable, stack material neatly in the plant, put tools back in order, ensure all parts have been reported to QC, all material used is reported to inventory, turn in material usage sheets and report any machinery problems to the production supervisor before leaving. The emphasis here is to minimize supplies waste.

52. **Assign minimum daily sales calls**: Assign a minimum number of sales calls to be made every day to each salesperson to be done before they leave for the day. Ask them what they are doing that someone else could do so they can sell. Ask them every day and teach those around sales to continue this tradition. Ask all of your salespeople, *"What do you have to do here that keeps you from obtaining more orders and earning more money?"*

53. **Daily brochures and handouts**: Have the receptionist put brochures out for all visitors in the front lobby. He or she should encourage everyone to take one or more with them. Have your truck drivers give all customers company brochures announcing new products, new services or new features that our company now offers. Drop them off on all new delivery routes or stops. Ask your quality control department to hand these out to visiting customers during audits. Ask your production personnel to have them available in the plant or in your warehouses to pass out to visitors. If they are small enough, stuff them in the invoices

that go to customers and in with the checks that go to vendors. Include all departments in selling. Their paychecks depend upon it.

54. **New customer mailers:** For every new customer set up during the day, research the names and addresses of all associated sister divisions and branches. Mail brochures offering corporate discounts to those locations and buyers. Have the salesperson tell the new buyer he can most likely get a further discount from your company if he can get his company's other buyers to also place orders with your company.

55. **Mail targeted advertisements every day:** Make sure to mail 20, 30 or 100 new advertisements, brochures, discount coupons or whatever mail that will gain new customers or will entice other potential customers to call for a quote. You pick the number to target every day but do it consistently no matter what. Make it a daily habit. Make sure your mailing inserts and brochures are up to date, relevant to the market, interesting to the potential reader and finally provoking enough to cause the recipient to call your firm. Place stickers on the outside of your mailers to invite the recipients to read the inserts and make it easy to call you anytime.

56. **Ask all new callers how they heard about the company.** Find out why customers called your

company. Whatever caused them to call, you need to repeat what you did correctly. Write down the reason stated by new callers when they call looking for a quote. Was it from a conversation they had with someone? Was it from literature from our company received in the mail? Was it from a sales call made by our salesperson? Was it from a referral by our current customers or vendors? If there is more than one answer, identify the main cause that provoked them to call. We need to acknowledge referrals and reward them. No matter what, find out what causes your company to obtain new customers.

57. **Ask salespeople what keeps them from selling:** Poll the salespeople why they cannot sell and do it every day. What stops them? What procedure do we have that stands in the way of getting new sales orders? What keeps them from finalizing and receiving a customer purchase order? What procedure or department does not work or hinders that salesperson from getting new business? Has anything happened in the market that dictates that our company must change to respond to the market? Has anything happened that will change our ability to get new orders or get orders out the door?

58. **Ask receiving people about returns**: Find out what products are being returned every day. What is wrong with our products that the customer determined they were not worth the cost or did not work as portrayed by our salespeople? Ask the

receiving people every day what has come back and the reasons for the return. (i.e. wrong color, bad finish, incorrect parts shipped, parts do not work, ruined product shipped to customer, delivery was late, product failed under the customer's QC plan, etc.) Also be sure to ask your receiving people what was received by the company that does NOT come through the Receiving Department but that was received in another office or company facility bypassing internal controls. This indicates missed internal controls (i.e. not checked for a company purchase order, not inspected by quality control personnel, not compared to an internal purchase order which helps to define characteristics or technical issues).

59. **Ask employees who/what holds them up every day:** Ask your employees what keeps them from doing their jobs or what daily processes, tasks or the normal routine cuts into their productivity. Ask what can be trimmed, reduced, cut. Ask what actions they currently perform do not work or work well. Ask what department seems to be running without direction, which company departments are constantly behind, holding up workflow, stopping billings, slowing shipping, etc. Ask the question because every employee will most likely have answers that are not yet known.

60. **Ask employees what about the company can be improved**: Pass out slips to all employees to find out what they think needs to be improved within the

company. If you wish, change the question to, "Where do you see the biggest waste that happens a lot in the company?" Invite them to cover anything they want but get their ideas back at the end of the first day. Let them talk about anything. They will fill your ears with plenty of items to work on challenging the company, some of which you were unaware.

61. **Add approval levels for spending**: If you need to cut your costs, assign a senior level of manager to approve spending in the purchasing department before monies are committed. Give him instructions for now that he is to stop any discretionary spending that does not support sales or production in some direct manner. His instructions should be to buy only critical items in order for sales and workflow to continue. If he has problems with understanding this, he too may be part of your company's overall cost problem.

62. **Most overtime worked result of internal problems**: Find out who worked the most overtime yesterday and why. What was another alternative that was not considered before having a man work 16 hours in production? Who was working and why? How many hours did they work? Was there any possibility that they could have gone home on normal time and finished the job the next day? Who determined for the employees to work 16 hours? Did the customer pay for this? Did anyone ask the customer this question?

63. **How many failures in quality control today**: Ask how many product failures were detected during the day and request the reasons. Any particular operators, shift, set of machines, specific difficult products? Any trends noted?

64. **How many customers were angry today**? Ask the receptionist about any angry customers? Ask if there were any and how they were handled. Ask him or her to keep a log of disgruntled customer buyers, phone numbers, contact names and time of the incidents. Does that receptionist know for a fact that the customer was handled with courtesy and got his question answered or his problem solved? If the receptionist does not know, follow this up to find out the procedure and how it worked within the sales department. If it did not work for the customer positively, assign the sales department to contact that customer to ensure he is satisfied with everything that happened subsequently to his order.

65. **Review your list of offsite records and destroy those records outside the legal limit**. If you keep company records offsite, print a complete listing of the boxes they hold and get rid of those outside the legal limit. Boxes containing tax records need only be retained for a set number of years. Customer purchase orders and contracts are to be retained for a set number of years. Find out what these legal limits are and destroy all boxes outside those

parameters. This will immediately cut your storage bill at this outside facility.

66. **Have an independent party review incoming bills to question spending**; Assign someone outside of purchasing and accounting to review incoming bills randomly. Rotate the responsibility through many various functions, quality control, maintenance, production supervisors or even your outside auditors. Invite all comments regarding validity of charges, appropriateness of spending, level of authorizations or volume of purchases.

19 Questions And Further Tips To Ask Your Employees Who Submit Good And Profitable Suggestions

Try these additional questions and approaches for your employees who want to participate:

1. How did you see your idea implemented?

2. Who in our company did you see that would implement your idea the best way or the most beneficial way for the company? How would they do it and when?

3. Do you see your idea taking a lot of time or effort?

4. How did you think the company could save money doing this?

5. What benefits would be derived from starting your idea tomorrow?

6. Who in the plant would you suggest do this?

7. Would another person have to be hired, or, does your idea cut labor costs?

8. If this cuts labor costs, how many hours per week does this eliminate?

9. How would this new procedure, new product, new regulation or new part number work?

10. Where do you think this equipment should be installed?

11. Do you have an idea what this device looks like?

12. Why do you think this new item or procedure would help or improve the product or the process?

13. **Interview the employee to fully understand what he was trying to convey.** When you do this, you get him interested in the answer and the ultimate solution. You also may get an answer that will save your firm $100,000 per year. (i.e. The person who recognized a laboratory failure realized that applying this sticky gooey mistake on the back of small pieces of paper would allow them to be stuck on the wall or surface, thus the birth of the post-it note.)

14. **Review all suggestions and talk to each employee.** You will not know until you begin the program so methodically read each and every suggestion and keep an open mind.

15. **Call every person who provided a suggestion and talk to them about their idea.** They may not have expressed it well on paper but may indeed have a potentially great idea.

16. **Be picky about who speaks with employees.** Make sure you are careful in selecting the people to speak with your employees; they need to be creative and open-minded or they will work against you projecting a negative attitude during the interviews.

17. **Do not use supervisors.** Do not use their supervisor regardless of how easy you think this may be to do. These employees do not want to talk to their supervisors only to have the discussion taint their relationship later during work. Many times, third party independent personnel are good because

they have no preconceived ideas working at odds against new ideas.

18. **Perform a second review of all suggestions after the first round is finished.** Do not restrict the review of ideas to only one or two people. Run them through another group of employees who work in entirely different parts of the company. Get different perspectives.

19. **Paying attention to employees is worth the effort.** You are doing yourself a great service, talking to employees five minutes because they are being regarded as important and that is not done often enough. As a side benefit, you may also get some great ideas for the company.

14 Questions To Ask Employees To Increase Your Product Offering And Increase Profits

Always remember that some of the best ideas are lying dormant within your employees. Unless you ask for them they have been taught to keep it to themselves and do their assigned jobs Poor managers or supervisors at work cut them off or ignore these suggestions which then causes those with ideas to be quiet and give up trying. You can change that quickly. Try a few or all of these questions to ask your employees about your current product offering and changes they would like to see.

Try these questions out to provoke great ideas from your employees at all levels:

1. Are there any products our company makes that you think we should expand or change (i.e. Different colors, different sizes, available with different components)?

2. Is there a way we can cut down or reduce our cost of packaging? Can you think of the worst item that requires hard to use or difficult packaging?

3. Do you see a way to cut down on the time it takes to finish a product?

4. Have you watched any machine that tears up or ruins products? Which machine was it? What did it do?

5. Do you know of faulty tooling, bad tools or old equipment that requires too long to use? Does it

cause the operator to ruin a product or leave marks or cause damage while it is being used?

6. Do you see a way to cut down the labor cost on assembly of any product?

7. Which product takes lots of people and requires a tremendous amount of time?

8. Which product that the company makes causes problems for other products? (i.e. product process leaves residue, oil or dirt or accumulated material behind, requires cleanout of the machine before another can be run, wear and tear causes the machine to need service, other particular or specific machine downtime problems due to the manufacture of this product).

9. Can you think of one process you know about that takes too long or needs something developed to speed it up? Have you thought of this while working in the past?

10. Have you noticed any product that we make that seems to take too long or takes too many people or seems to use too much material?

11. Was there any product that seems outdated or needs to be rejuvenated? (i.e. upgrade taste on food or drink products, add a new flavor for a food, add a new color for a paper product or ink pen, add a new beautiful cover or faster charger or easy carrying case to the purchase)

12. If you had to identify one thing or one area to improve in the facility where you work, what should we change?

13. What can we add to make our products more useable, fun, easy to handle, more pliable, more pleasant to hold, more attractive, lighter weight, more flexible, more durable, longer lasting, brighter, more luxurious, less noisy, less rough, smoother, more desirable to women, more desirable to men, more exciting for children or some other feature applicable to your company's marketing strategy?

14. What one thing are we doing wrong?

Remember to tell the employees that their best ideas will be eligible for a financial payout through the suggestion box program.

10 Questions To Ask All Employees About Utilities Waste

There is far more waste in the utility bills than most realize (i.e. water, sewer, electricity, natural gas, bottled gas, etc.) Most employees know about utility waste from their own experience at home. Here are some questions to ask everyone about how they think the company may save on the company's utilities expense.

1. Do you have any ideas about how can we cut our electric bill? If you had to pay for our light bill, where would you cut first? Where do we waste money?

2. Can you think of a place or department where machines run unnecessarily when they should be turned off? If you are not sure, what is your gut feel?

3. Are there any machines that can be programmed to turn off or reduce speeds when not being used? Can a programmable device be used to accomplish this? (i.e. similar to turning off home lights when one is away at the office)

4. Can you think of a place or department where lights are unnecessarily on all of the time? What specific areas need attention? Describe the details to support your answer.

5. Do you think we waste electricity or gas, and if yes, where in the plant specifically? Describe the production line, machine, area of the plant, an isolated building or maybe the level of loading may need to be discussed.

6. Have we had an analysis of our electricity usage?

7. Do we have frequent outages? Does the rest of the neighborhood have the same recurring problem or is it an issue with our own facilities?

8. Do we water the lawn, flowers, shrubs or trees too much? Do the sprinklers seem to be on at the wrong time, or too long, or do they not work and most goes down the drain?

9. Do the toilets or urinals run too much? Excessively?

10. Do we water the grass on the days it is raining? Does anyone know how to turn this off for the day? Has anyone trained you to divert this program?

10 Questions To Ask All Employees About Supplies Waste

All employees know something about excess usage or waste that they notice in the plant or office where they work every day. Ask them one or more of these questions about where to save on supplies expense. Consider putting the questions in with their paychecks and offering some prizes for the best and most lucrative suggestions.

1. If you had to tell me one item where we waste the most money on supplies, what would it be? Why do you say this?

2. How can we cut down on the amount of supplies used? Why do you say we can cut the amount used?

3. Which of our supplies that we buy are wasted? How do you know that? Describe how we waste or overkill the use of specific supplies.

4. Do we buy the wrong supplies? Why do you say this and why do you think you are right?

5. Do we have old supplies that were ordered and never used? Tell me where they are so we can see if we can return them.

6. Do we have problems with supplies that go missing on a regular basis? Which ones can you think of that turn up gone?

7. Do you see supplies leave with employees? Do you care to share names or at least let us know where to look the next time? Your comments are confidential.

8. Would you buy supplies that are bought now if you had to get two different upper managers to sign off on the purchase? If not, does this not tell you something about the need for these items? Why would you not ask if you had to get approvals?

9. What supplies do you think we buy that are unnecessary? What specifically makes you think and say this?

10. Did you know our company can return defective supplies if we discover them after receiving them? Have you ever found supplies that were no good and you did not report them to purchasing?

15 Questions To Ask All Production Workers About Production Loss Or Waste

Here are some questions you can select from to ask your plant personnel and machine operators who see what goes wrong every day. They may have been suggesting ideas for a long time and no one above their supervisor listened. If you like submit them with their paychecks and tell them they are welcome to keep answers anonymous or private.

1. What is wrong with this machine that you operate (you fill in the name)?

2. Does this machine your run operate without any problems and if no, why not?

3. What does this machine do that causes problems or causes unplanned scrap or flaws?

4. Does the machine break down a lot?

5. Have you been trained on this machine like you would like? Do you need further training?

6. Does this machine act up? Does it stall? Is it easy or hard to perform an initial setup?

7. Does it destroy product or cause problems for some parts?

8. Do you know what signs to look for before calling maintenance personnel?

9. Does it get serviced on a normal basis?

10. Do our maintenance people seem to know how to fix it or not?

11. Is there an operator who abuses the machine or needs training?

12. What are the pinch-points in the plant that you have seen and witnessed that significantly jam things up?

13. Where are these pinch-points located and at what times of the day or evening do these areas interrupt the normal smooth flow of operations?

14. Describe the top three backlogs or jam-ups that occur during a typical day? What do you suggest to resolve these problems?

15. Who needs to take production backlogs more seriously than they currently do? Please mention the person or function who or which can reduce the frequency of these shutdowns during the shift.

22 Chronological Steps For A Sales Order To Go Through Your Company

The best training you can give your new employees along with their orientation is to teach how a sales order goes through the company. Tell them they can expedite orders by being aware how the process works and pointing out when something is stopped or not working. Their efforts ensure more sales which ensures hopefully more profits which in the end results in enough money to give out as company bonuses to the employees.

Here is a general example of how a sales order goes through one manufacturing company (from initial order to collection results).

1. **Customer considers your firm's capabilities.** The customer may find your firm on the internet, in a trade show or featured on one of those flyers you had made that you thought no one read. Something causes the customer to consider your firm and he decides to try you. This is one aspect that is lost in sales and marketing. "Where did you see us first and what caused you to ultimately call us?" Hardly anyone asks this question in order to understand the success and payoff of various types of advertising and marketing materials. Which one worked and which ones do not work? Which costly marketing dollars spent were effective and which were not?

2. **Customer decides to contact your firm.** The customer does one of these things: he either calls your company, emails a request for quote to an employee or distributor or faxes a RFQ (request for

quote) to the sales department fax machine or company online help email address. He may or may not actually talk to someone at this point. This is where someone in your firm needs to contact this new potential customer immediately. Show your responsiveness and call him. This is another reason to watch the fax machine, watch your email constantly and even be careful and watch the incoming snail mail. Teach the receptionist to protect all customer inquiries. This all seems pretty evident on the surface but say it loudly and firmly anyway.

3. **Customer calls your firm.** The customer reaches your switchboard, asks for the sales department and is transferred. In certain industries, the firm may require that you answer every telephone call personally if it is known that your buyers expect personal attention. If it is not impossible, why would you not talk to someone who might give you a $25,000 order? This whole process involves training the operator. That person needs to know exactly what to do for a number of situations. What is the next step to take when everyone in the sales department is busy? Who should be called, paged, or personally notified? At what time specifically is it ok to break in on meetings or to knock on closed doors in order to get someone in sales to take an urgent call? Spell these answers out clearly in writing.

4. **Customer gets a 'live' voice or a recording machine?** When the customer is indeed

transferred, does he get a live person or voicemail? How many times is it necessary for him to call back and ask for a sales person? What is your company policy about this and what do you want the operator to do? Did that person offer to page the sales person to try to get him to take the call? Find out and correct any gaps in this policy today. Regardless of what happens, teach your operator to get a number and a name in case the call is lost and vow to return the call to him within 5 or 10 minutes. Prove to the customer that their call is important and follow up.

5. **Customer describes what they want to buy, have made or have serviced.** The customer sends a blueprint, written description or a copy of an existing product and asks for a quote for manufacturing more, ordering more, providing a service, etc. At this point, does the customer get to speak to someone live on the telephone? Is there a return call to inform him the print or written instructions have been received and can be read or poses problems or raises question for clarification? If the guy calls back and tells the receptionist that he can't get anyone to call him back, what does she do at this critical point? Create these procedures, teach each of the parties involved and make it effective right away; your business depends upon it.

6. **The customer bid is forwarded to the estimator/bid dept.** Inside sales and estimating figure a cost and send back a quote to the customer. Do the sales personnel actually speak to the

customer or do they just send the bid response back via email? It makes a difference and the way it is handled may make or lose the bid. Why? If the company bid is only a small dollar amount from the lowest bid, the customer's buyer might tip our company off to this trying to favor us. If we do not talk to him, he cannot do this on behalf of our company. If no one speaks to the customer, no one will know the bid situation and thus may lose out on an opportunity. A human voice can be convincing when the customer truly wants another company to bid on its work. Call the customer back and show them you are genuinely interested in the work. Demonstrate to them you want the job. When you do not personalize your response, you are regarded as fat and lazy and just another big company or a poorly run firm and who wants to deal with that? Remember that the time you call may be the day they give you the job after submitting multiple previous bids.

7. **Request customer information for granting credit.** The inside sales group at this point will ask the customer to submit either a credit application or simply request credit information that most firms have readily available (i.e. bank contact information, company address, Duns number, addresses, telephone, fax, email addresses and a multitude of credit references with telephone numbers and contact names of those who know this company).

8. **Customer credit established**. The sales group at this point asks accounting or your credit department to get this new customer approved for credit terms if possible. This goes with the bid that will go back to the client. Do the people in accounting know how quickly they are to respond? (i.e. one business day, four hours, two weeks, etc.) If they do not, tell them their responsibility. They can file later; tell them you need their participation on granting credit as soon as possible.

9. **Does the company respond in a timely and professional manner?** How quickly do you respond? Does the potential customer know how long it will take to get an answer back from your firm? Do you tell him upfront what to expect? Who is responsible for this? What does it tell you if the receptionist states a caller complains he sent in a request for a quote and no one ever called him back and it has now been three days? Ask specifically to see if this ever occurs. Follow up on this gap in your system procedure. You may have to assign a lead in your sales department to capture and log in all requests for quotes (RFQs) in order to see how long they have been sitting without a response from your firm.

10. **Customer decides to place an order with your firm.** The client sends a purchase order to your inside sales. What happens after this occurs? Does anyone pay attention to the guy that just hands your company an order? Does he get thanked or does anyone show appreciation from your company? If

the answer is no, you have problems within your sales department that need attention now. Someone needs to acknowledge the order and commit to a delivery date if it is not mentioned clearly on the purchase order. Someone also needs to personally say, "Thank you for your order today. We appreciate it!" Remember that this is not done with an email.

11. **Due date established with purchase order.** At this point, the customer is fully expecting your firm to ship their order to them by an official due date. This due date changes if the customer changes, falters or alters the order in any way and those changes affect the time schedule. Your firm must tell the customer every time the due date changes in writing and on the telephone with the reason for the delay.

12. **Your firm personally thanks the customer, or does it?** Does anyone call and talk to the buyer after he awarded your company a purchase order? Did anyone thank him personally on the telephone? Does anyone know what size potential this job is or if it represents a small piece of a much bigger project? Do we have any idea how large this client can potentially become?

13. **Bid or Quote turns into a sales order - moves to production/ purchasing.** Inside sales personnel hand the job to production and purchasing. Inside sales forwards job instructions to plant personnel to produce. Is there any check and balance at this point to ensure the order is complete and the firm is

expected to make a minimum required net profit % on the job? Is there a secondary check on the bid?

14. **Material and outside services ordered through purchase orders for this job.** Are material or services pinch points for your firm? There are lead times on material or procuring outside services so those purchase orders need to be issued first. Many times nothing can start until material arrives. Purchasing should respond within a standard time deadline. (i.e. One business day, 48 hours, etc.)

15. **Material in, production scheduled.** Production schedules machines and purchasing buys material. Either department notifies inside sales when there are known delays that will occur.

16. **Production now projected late.** The customer needs to be notified immediately when the given original due date is going to be delayed whether it is the fault of the customer (late delivery of supplied material or blueprints) or the fault of your firm (delayed production). Is this notification done automatically through an email or on the telephone personally? Does someone make sure to get a formal acknowledgment from the customer's buyer about the shipping delay? A signed acknowledgement is good backup if needed later in court. If nothing signed comes back, you need an email reply or acceptance at a minimum for your audit trail.

17. **Shipping ships parts to customer.** If it is the customer's truck, does the shipping department go

out of its way to be helpful to that trucker? If your firm is shipping the order to the customer, does someone call or email in advance to notify the buyer his order is on the way? If that buyer is located in another facility, does anyone notify him of the shipment ahead of time or at least once it has been delivered?

18. **Customer is shorted.** Customer receives your shipment, states that his order count is received but the quantity is deficient by one part at this point. What does your inside sales department do when notified a vital shipment is short?

19. **Replacement shortage is produced and shipped to customer at no charge.** How does your firm handle production shortages found after shipping? Do your people respond quickly to the customer? Do they have other parts on hand to ship? Do they stay after hours in order to fix problems or to help the customer through a problem?

20. **Billings sends invoice.** Your billings department emails, mails or faxes the invoice to the customer. Any or all of these options is up to the customer and what they prefer. Sometimes once the customer gets an invoice in the mail and there is a reported problem, they may call and state there are problems with the shipment. They typically state they cannot pay the invoice since the shipment was short, billed incorrectly, rejected or failed for some other reason. Do your employees know what to do in case of these failures?

21. **Customer will not pay your invoice due to shipment errors, pricing problems, defective products or lousy deficient service**. Your billings personnel should immediately notify the sales department of notifications received from companies that refuse to pay invoices due to various failures. Someone in sales needs to attempt to resolve this problem with the customer in order to get the company paid on the questionable shipped parts. All of the negotiations with outside customers need to stem from sales personnel and not from any other department.

22. **Customer unable to pay bill.** Sometimes the customer does not have the money to pay the bill. At this point, credit personnel attempt to get a payment plan put into place and mutually agreed upon. Your firm should be on the telephone with the customer constantly in order to get some reimbursement from the unpaid invoices up until those invoices are finally handed over to your internal lawyer (demand letter) and then given to an outside collection firm which will take legal action applicable to your state and municipality laws along with a hefty percentage of the eventual payment extracted by the court. (i.e. 25 to 50%, depending upon age of invoice).

26 Sample Documents To Include Chronologically In A Company Training Manual

In order to train new employees, it is helpful to show them examples of company documents so they recognize these forms. Here is a chronological listing of 26 sample documents you might start with to create your own company manual. Add or subtract whatever fits your needs.

1. Customer RFQs (requests for quotes received from outside clients).

2. Company quotes on letterhead dated and addressed to the buyer (pricing at various volume levels, who pays freight, applicable taxes and levels of warranty).

3. Customer purchase orders (include three or four examples from different companies for comparison).

4. Internal production or job orders (orders created from customer purchase orders which are sent to the plant to make or pick products to ship for a client).

5. Material usage sheets (material picked and assigned to orders or jobs (job cost system).

6. Time card labor sheet (hand sign-on, electronic clock in labor costs on jobs for manufacturing).

7. Quality control approval (date approved and signed for release according to customers' specifications).

8. Quality control approval to ship to customer.

9. Company packing list. (company list of each part number and number of items included in the shipment).

10. Company bill of lading.

11. Company invoice issued to customers (quantity of parts shipped, price each, freight costs, taxes, handling costs).

12. Signed delivery tickets (proof of delivery to the customer) provided by a signature of the customer's receiving department, a third-party freight company (FedEx, DHL, UPS).

13. Company warranty accompanying all new purchases.

14. Accounts receivable statement (list of all outstanding unpaid customer invoices aged by invoice date based upon the credit terms granted this customer), normally sent out to the customer after the invoice has been received and entered by the customer.

15. Bank notification of incoming wire (cash received, invoice paid).

16. Bank notification of lock box receipts (customer checks are received, cashed and monies deposited at your bank in the account of your firm).

17. Bank statement for lockbox at month-end.

18. Bank statement for checking account at month-end.

19. Bank statement for CDs, savings, sweep accounts or any other bank instrument in the company name.

20. Bank statement for lockbox fees, usage fees, etc.

21. Accounts Payable Aging (list of all unpaid AP invoices sorted by vendor).

22. Accounts Receivable Aging (list of all unpaid AR invoices sorted by customer).

23. Electric bill example.

24. Telephone bill example.

25. Credit card summary bill example.

26. Property tax bills (normally semi-annual or annual bills).

Suggestion: One method to get a company training manual put together quickly is to ask all employees to submit their copies by the end of the day of all the documents that pass through their desk or email every day.

20 Examples Of Business And Professional Courtesy

One of the best methods to teach your employees business and professional courtesy is to give them examples to demonstrate how they are to do their job. Here are some examples you might start with as a base to add or subtract those important in your specific company.

1. **Admitting company errors.** Oh, sir, you are correct and I am wrong. That price is posted incorrectly for that item. This is one instance where I am allowed to charge the incorrect lower price for you, when it is our fault. Let me ring that up now and honor the price posted as you saw it. (It will not hurt to allow incorrect pricing errors for items under a specified small dollar amount cutoff; give your salesclerks the freedom to do this for your customers. The customers will not forget and the price errors will be offset by good customer relations.)

2. **Product complaints.** Please tell me the problem with our product and I will do what I can to resolve the problem. I appreciate the fact you came back to the store. I will make sure we get this resolved to your satisfaction while you are here. (Understand the loyalty of a customer that returns rather than going to a competitor. Realize the possible long term sales opportunities that lie waiting if you can make a customer happy by giving in a little.)

3. **Customer assurance of full warranty.** Please try this solution and if it does not work for you, bring it

back in for a full refund. Ask for me, Julie. I will personally take care of it for you. There will not be any problem returning it or if you wish, exchanging it for a different selection. We will work this out for you. (Personalize the conversation; give a personal name and tell the customer ahead of time what to expect.)

4. **Limited sales and honoring customer loyalty.** Thank for your calling us about our special. Our sale ends at the close of business today. I see here in our system you have been a customer for over ten years. I do not know when the next sale might be. You know if you cannot come in today, I would be glad to go right now when I hang up and reserve one of the remaining sale items for you if you wish. You can come in over the next couple of days when you are able to pick it up. We do appreciate your business. Let me know if I can do that for you.

5. **Helping customers.** Thank you for calling ABC Company sir. I'm sorry you lost your wallet; I want to help you locate it. If you will give me some identifying marks or contents of the wallet you lost, I will check one that a customer just turned in here at "Lost and Found". Please tell me something unique about it if you do not mind, such as color, specific marking or lettering.

6. **Professional departments.** Hello, this is Frank Smith in Quality Control. May I help you? (Identify the department and who is talking to exude customer service even within the organization)

7. **Company greeting.** Good morning! ABC Corporation. How may I help you today? (Be pleasant, identify the company and ask what you can do for them, and mean it.)

8. **Company greeting and courtesy.** Good morning, this is ABC Corp., may I put you on hold for just a moment? (Ask politely versus cutting off the caller. If this does not work, try because the lines get clogged, try this: "Good morning, this ABC Corp., please hold and I will be right with you.")

9. **Professional departments.** Accounting, this is Donald Smith in Accounts Payable. May I help you? (Identify the department, the individual and maybe a title and then ask what you can do for the customer, always.)

10. **Returned call.** I am sorry that Mr. Adams did not answer his telephone. Would you like to leave a voicemail or if you prefer, tell me your name and telephone number and I will see to it that he calls you back concerning your complaint. What would you prefer? (Do something no other receptionist does; offer to take a personal message. This is rare and will be memorable to the customer.)

11. **Correcting service problems.** I am sorry you had problems with our service provided this morning. If you tell me what was not done to your satisfaction, I will let the crew management know and they will send a different group out to finish the job to your satisfaction. If you tell me that it is alright and acceptable to you, I will see to it they come and

check with you before they leave to make sure you are satisfied with their work. This will be done at no additional cost to you. Does that seem like that will take care of your needs? (Realize when a paying customer complains, he is saying, "I am willing to give you a second chance so you have this one chance to keep my business. It is yours to lose.")

12. **Lobby and front desk courtesy.** If you will have a seat for a few minutes, I will tell Mr. Anderson you are here to see him. If he does not get back with me in that time, I will call him again for you.

13. **Lobby and front desk courtesy (follow-up after a short wait).** Sir, I know you have been waiting for several minutes. I want you to know I have called Mr. Anderson about your appointment. I told him you arrived early and are still patiently waiting. He told me to tell you he will be with you within five minutes and he does apologize for the delay.

14. **Delivery man courtesy.** Hello, this is Derek with ABC Corporation. I am delivering your order today and I am in front of your house at 11405 White Oak Lane. It is raining right now and this is a large package wrapped in a cardboard box. I am calling you on the number you left with our customer service department phone because I wanted to be sure that I can leave this package for you on the back porch. If you wish, I can take it back to the store and you can pick it up at the store between 7 am and 7 pm, Monday through Saturday. It is your decision. What would you like?

15. **Personal customer service.** I am sorry you had problems reaching customer service. Here is another direct toll free number that generally has less traffic and if that does not work, here, also, is my direct telephone number to call if all else fails. If the other number that I give you does not work, you are welcome to call me, I will be happy to make sure it gets done for you.

16. **Website customer service.** Tell me what you were looking for on our website and I will find it for you. We make note when our customers cannot find items and will make changes when the website does not work for the benefit of the customer. Do you remember anything about the product name? (Be helpful and find out how the programming of your firm's website is flawed, not user friendly and detrimental to your company image. Customers will tell you what is wrong and you will be glad to listen since they may only tell you once frustrated with their worthless data searches.)

17. **Billing information/customer service.** If you give me your name or account number, I will find your information in our system and check to make sure we have the correct mailing address and a good billing date if the current one is not convenient for you. I am sorry your payment envelope was returned to you; we will do whatever it takes today to get this resolved.

18. **Customer service for customer loyalty.** If you give me your name and telephone number, I will find this product in our stores and call you back to

let you know if we have it in stock. If we have it in stock and you wish, we can send it to you ground-shipping. Because this is the first time you have tried to buy online according to our records, and because you have had an account with us for ten years, I will ship it overnight at no additional cost to you. May I do that for you today to show our appreciation for being a loyal customer? (Acknowledge the customer's years of business and loyalty, one good benefit derived from maintaining clean good customer records.)

19. **Handling customer service complaints and follow-up.** Tell me who you had problems with and we will speak with that customer service representative for you. If you wish, give me your number and once I locate the representative, secure a credit for your account and ensure all new shipments are going out, I will call you. I will try to get that done today, but, that may not take place until tomorrow morning because it is already 2 p.m. Is that ok with you? (A display of courtesy, a specific goal stated in behalf of the customer and a question to ensure the proposal is agreed to by the customer all add up to great customer relations.)

20. **Courteous delay.** Good morning! I am working with another customer this minute, but I promise to return to your call in just a few moments if you will hang on for a few moments. (Immediately impress someone when they enter the building, lobby and let them know you are busy, but you will be helping them in a few moments.)

18 Employee Payroll Benefits

All employees need to see the list of all payroll and work benefits that are paid in their behalf. They may pay for some items but this list generally covers most benefit plans offered by companies. You also need to take into consideration the cost of all of these items when costing out jobs and measuring profitability.

Have your list for your company available to hand out to your employees when asked.

1. Vacation pay (use the average pay rate plus a reasonable amount of overtime).

2. Sick pay (use the average annual salary in the plant or office and apply the amount of days allowed in your policy.

3. Jury duty (use the average annual salary and apply the amount of days allowed in your policy).

4. FUTA (federal unemployment insurance, use the company overall salary average and the assigned rate to derive this employer cost).

5. SUTA (state unemployment insurance, use the company overall salary average and assigned rate to derive this employer cost).

6. Workers' Compensation Insurance (use the overall premium average divided by the number of employees, a mixed rate).

7. Life insurance (use a salary average amount times the premium of an average-aged worker).

8. Short term disability (use a salary average to select a coverage premium).

9. Long term disability (use a salary average to select a coverage premium).

10. Medical insurance (use a family rate for comparison purposes).

11. Dental insurance (use a family rate).

12. Uniforms and shoes if supplied (use an average).

13. Paid lunchtime and break time (use a salary/hourly average).

14. Pension expense (use a salary average).

15. #401K matching expense (mention vesting period of time and assume fully vested cost).

16. Discounts offered through nearby businesses in association with your company offered to your employees.

17. Training / certification expenses (i.e. machine operators on new equipment, safety training, forklift training, accounting training for bank software).

18. Tuition reimbursement if offered (display a weighted average).

9 Issues For The Receptionist To Note And Report Daily

1. **Hard to get sales people to answer?** Do incoming calls from customers always get personally answered by a sales person? Your customers need a personal touch; they want to speak to someone and this is an advantage you have with a live operator. Your customers got this far to a live person so do not let them down now and push them into a voicemail system. Get someone to answer the telephone. Do not ignore this service attribute. Do not allow calls to go to voicemail when the customer wants to speak with a voice.

2. **Sales calls go into voicemail?** Is there anyone in the sales department that will not take calls or forces calls into voicemail? Does the receptionist have problems with any one individual answering the telephone or calling customers back? If unknown, keep a log and review it weekly.

3. **Customer complaints go unanswered?** Do the customer complaints which do not get a call back from your inside sales people forwarded or noted to the manager in charge? Does anyone ultimately get back with the customer?
   Suggestion: Encourage the receptionist to stay on the telephone until an irate customer call gets personally answered by a sales representative. She can also take the customer's number to make sure she does not lose him. Inform everyone in sales

that they are to pick up the telephone when she is paging for help.

4. **Purchasing will not take calls to get competitive bidders?** Are there problems getting purchasing to take calls from vendors? *Note: Your purchasing or procurement manager needs to review buyer priorities. Evidence of this may insinuate internal control problems.*

5. **Customer irate waiting for sales people?** Is it difficult to find sales personnel when a customer refuses voicemail and states emphatically they want to speak with someone? *Note: Why is this request by a customer such a problem? Someone is responsible for all incoming calls in the sales department. Who is not doing their job?*

6. **Vendors calling to get paid?** Are there numerous vendor collection calls to accounts payable seeking payment? *Note: Collection calls continuously clogging up the switchboard obviously insinuates the company is not paying bills on time.*

7. **Absence of supervisors or managers – no one in charge?** Is there a time during the workday or a specific period when a supervisor or manager is gone that problems begin (regardless of the department or function)? Receptionists will recognize these patterns and need to report an increase of problems when this occurs.

8. **Human resources not available for employees?** Are there a number of calls from employees to human resources that do not get answered or get

returned? *Note: This is bad for employee relations and needs to be corrected for the sake of your employees.*

9. **Employees out of the office hard to contact?** Are telephone calls made to employees on the road frequently unanswered? Receptionists are many times responsible to call sales personnel, company truck drivers, department managers or just anyone that is currently out of the company facilities. Is there anyone of that is consistently difficult to contact, slow to call back or is known never to call back?

The receptionist is never expected to know all of the ramifications of problems incurred with incoming telephone calls, but it is well worth asking these questions and more. Train this person to note problems and ask customer questions to ensure they are satisfied with reaching their inside sales personnel as well as any other department requested. Your receptionist is the first voice your customers hear so make it a pleasant and helpful one.

8 Immediate Benefits of Teaching Employees To Professionally Answer Their Company Telephone

Teach all of your employees to answer their extension and company cell phone professionally and courteously. Customers should never guess who answered the telephone.

Examples of standard company greetings given by all your employees:

"Hello, this is Frank Tully. May I help you?" (This call was directed through the switchboard so repeating the company name is not necessary.)

"Hello, this is ABC Store, Quality Department. This is Angeles, may I help you?" (This employee has a direct line so it is necessary to identify to the caller that he has called the right company. Reassure him; he is paying you.)

"Hello, this is William Sylva in Production. May I help you?" (This call directed through the switchboard so the caller knows he called the correct company.)

Yes, it will take a little time to get everyone on board, but your customers will notice. Have someone go from telephone extension to extension and randomly call employees to get them on board. Remind them of your courtesy program again and thank them in their paychecks. Remind your employees that anyone calling into the company could be looking to spend $1M so act like every call is worth $1M.

Benefits of a standardized friendly greeting include the following:

1. If you successfully put this standardized procedure into place, your customers will notice and appreciate the friendly approach.

2. Customers will automatically think that customer service is better, even if it is not. They become used to the professional attitude and come to expect it. Once they have heard all of your people be professional on the telephone, they will come to expect it and notice how other firms lack that discipline. You will shame the competition.

3. Customers will appreciate getting someone who at least seems to be willing to help them. Make it worth calling your firm. If you have some employees who just cannot seem to be helpful, you need new employees; replace them and do not look back. They are far more detrimental than you realize.

4. Your employees will make your competition look bad immediately. This is great for your business.

5. Your friendliness is catching. Your employees will like that the customers warm up to this. This is easy and becomes contagious and most importantly, differentiates your firm from the rest, if you can keep it going.

6. You want more business, so when your customers call you, you want them to have a great experience dealing with everyone in your firm. You do not want your employees to turn them off, so train your employees about this program starting today. Give them positive feedback heard from the clients about

this program. Tell them their friendliness is working and it does 'payoff' financially.

7. The first person you train is the receptionist who will speak to every one of your customers at least once. Make sure he or she does it well and conveys the image you want for your firm.

8. Make sure that top management answers the telephone as nicely as your great receptionist. If they do not, be pleasant when you remind them.

13 Typical Employee "What If" Questions To Answer For Training

Part of training employees is to tell them what to do when things go wrong or unexpected problems or issues occur. The best way to do this is ask for your employees to ask questions they are unsure of and include the training for these solutions for future employees along with current ones.

1. What if we are shorthanded in the store? What do you want me to do to cover for the shortage in people? Who substitutes for whom and is there any pay difference paid in those circumstances? (HR and personnel policies.)

2. What if (employee name) does not show up on time to relieve me at the end of the shift? What do you want me to do? How long do you want me to wait and are we paid overtime? Do I need to call and notify someone after a certain amount of time waiting?

3. What if a customer tries to negotiate a price (in the store, in the field, in the warehouse, on the telephone, etc.)? Do I as a salesperson have any authority to change pricing? If so, how much dollar-wise, percentage each or percentage of the total? Does it make any difference on a $1.00 item? Does it make any difference if the dollar amount he offered was $10,000 for an $11,000 item? What are the break points in our company policy, if any? Do you want me to call anyone first before turning an offer away? The customer most likely will not try

to return again and try to negotiate if not given any answer since there are plenty of other stores to try.

4. What if I have to work a paid holiday? How am I paid? Do I get time off at another time? (HR and personnel payment policies.)

5. What if a customer says he will buy the (product) but will only do so if we extend the warranty by two more years? Are we willing to do this? Who do I ask to clear this approval or denial?

6. What if call in sick? Who do I call, when do I call and then after returning, how do I apply to take a paid sick day? Who has to sign or approve?

7. What if I cannot perform or learn the skills of the job? How long do I have once I have been hired before I am terminated?

8. What if the person training me does not do a good job? May I discuss this with someone?

9. What if I know or am aware of theft or illegal activity by other employees of the business? How can I disclose this anonymously? What if I do not want to be involved other than reporting it? I do not want to stir up problems with this specific employee so can my anonymity be guaranteed?

10. What if I have troubles with other personnel harassing me, or notice others bothering other employees? Who do I report this to?

11. What if I have problems understanding a customer on the telephone? Who can I call as a backup?

12. What if my computer locks up during data entry? Who do you want me to call or do you want me to reboot the system or stay out of it?

13. What if I am approached by a vendor who tries to give me money in order for our company to choose his goods or services? Who do I tell this to or do you want me to tell anyone? What is the company policy about this?

24 Typical Customer "What Ifs" Questions To Answer For Training

Your inside sales personnel who have answered many calls from confused or angry customers will be able to provide 75% of these questions concerning your company. Ask current and future customers to answer a simple "What if....." card you hand them and add the new representatives to your FAQ section of your website.

Examples of the questions customers ask:

1. What if my (product) fails to operate when I get home or it fails over the next few days. (Address with warranty information, return policy.)

2. What if I come into your store and cannot locate any immediate help working the floor? I realize your business is 'help yourself' but who do I ask that works there?

3. What if the finish comes off or is marred or wears off prematurely? What are my options to get it fixed? Are there any warranties for this potential problem?

4. What if some of the same products on your shelf are marked lower than others on the shelf? Do you honor those lower prices?

5. What if I cannot pay the layaway charges on time? What happens and what is the minimum I must pay to ensure I get to buy the layaway item?

6. What if I want to extend my product warranty beyond the normal one year? How do I do that? Who do I speak to or who do I call? How much

will it cost or is it available? Can it be billed monthly?

7. What if the color that you matched for me is not the right color in my home?

8. What if I am dissatisfied with the installers you sent to my house? Who may I talk to about this problem?

9. What if this does not fit my (you fill this in)? What are my options?

10. What if I am missing the instruction manual when I get home?

11. What if I do not have the internet at home? Is there an 800 number I can call and place an order?

12. What if your website connection does not work? What are my options?

13. What if I need training to operate this (computer hardware, computer software, appliance, machine, electronic device, smartphone, printer, etc.)? Do you have any classes offered or know of any?

14. What if I cannot find the replacement (oil, filters, parts, etc.) in my (town, local store, area)? Is there an alternative 800 number where I can order spare or replacement parts and have them delivered through expedited mail?

15. What if you advertised a product for sale and I cannot find it in the store? Who can help me or who in your organization may I call?

16. What if I get home and realize you have overcharged me when I review my receipt? Who do I speak to, call or visit?

17. What if I have problems in your firm's parking lot? Is there security? Who do I call or speak with?

18. What if my product works well but is no longer manufactured? Who do I call for repair or is that even an option?

19. What if the product I bought is recalled by the manufacturer? Who do I call at your store or are you aware of recalls? If you are not, who do you suggest I speak with?

20. What if this (product) does not fit my (various) that I have at home? (Discuss and reassure with your 100% satisfaction guarantee return policy.)

21. What if I cannot get this (product) to start, operate correctly, turn on, warm up, turn over, etc.? (Review 24/7 customer service support, online instruction manual download, troubleshooting guide.)

22. What if while operating your (device, machine, and product) I break down some late evening or working out of town or even out of state? Who do I call and will they answer? (Customer service telephone number and support team procedures.)

23. What if I notice one of your employees stealing? Is there a private or anonymous telephone number I can contact to report this? I do not want to be involved with this investigation but I am willing to

notify you of it if you tell me how to report unauthorized activity.

24. What if I want to pay my store credit card balance off in cash today? Is there any bonus or discount given to customers who are never late with payments? Do you reward good customers or only penalize bad ones? (This is a good question for any company. Do you

Ask "How Long" It Requires For These 27 Critical Tasks To Improve Profits

Study the length of time it takes for employees to react to various situations and you will find many opportunities to improve customer service, increase sales, cut costs and boost your bottom line. Start measuring these items daily and you will quickly see where your roadblocks stand in your company's process.

1. **How long to complete customers' billings to get invoices out?** Instruct the person who prepares the company invoices to cut and mail (email, fax) them by noon the following business day (i.e. 10:00 a.m. The next business day, 12 noon the next day, 3:00 p.m. The next business day --- you pick the time and what is feasible). You want invoices in front of customers in a timely manner because most vendors extended credit will not start the clock until they receive a bill. Speed it up. Streamline the process. The earlier most of these customers get their invoices, the faster you will be paid. Establish a deadline for this critical task regardless of where the information comes (i.e. One shipping department, fifteen remote warehouses, three countries, fourteen states, etc.). For this position, invoicing comes first. All extraneous non-important tasks can be done later. Do not make the mistake thinking that the right priorities will occur. Most clerks see all tasks as equal until trained otherwise. Review them now and ask what your employees

to rank their priority to ensure they fully understand which are the most important.

2. **How long to produce your product/perform your service?** Determine and measure the time required to make, select and pickup material, feed it into a machine, produce one part, remove it, clean it and stack it on a pallet ready to ship to a customer (i.e. You substitute the direct labor or production task specific for your company). It is not only critical to determine this time allowed, it is absolutely necessary to clearly state to your laborer what is expected; how much in what amount of time. If you do not get a concurrence, your measurement is useless because he does not buy in. Run test periods and dry runs. Try various setups and ask for input to cut the time required. Ensure the laborer is trained and the equipment is working as expected.

3. **How long to answer the telephone for anyone including customers?** How long does it take before a customer can actually reach someone in your organization? How long does it take to spend money in your firm? How difficult is it? Determine a standard and assign it to the receptionist and anyone else answering incoming calls. Respond within three rings or five rings or use secondary backup receptionists if necessary; develop a telephone system with the ability to be answered at multiple desks during busy times. If your firm develops a firm policy that clearly states calls will be answered within a determined time frame make sure the

group knows to fill in when volume of calls is higher than normal. Develop alternative logs in the event personnel are busy, away from their desk, out for the day or the call is from a new potential customer. In other words, know who to contact when the first employee is out. Write up these alternatives for each sales person and make that department update this **alternative answer plan** often.

4. **How long to distribute the mail?** How long does it take before company mail is gathered and distributed throughout the company? Answer this by asking what is received by mail these days? Are customers still sending checks directly to your firm? If that is so, assign the mail to be opened, date stamped, sorted and distributed by 9:00 a.m. (i.e. you pick the time for your own firm). For manual checks, get a check scanner for your office (if it makes economic sense, monthly cost versus gas to go to the bank).

5. **How long to ship a customer sales order?** How long does it take to load one full size delivery truck, verify the pallet count, verify shrink-wrap, packing list details and other pertinent information? You determine this, but set a time limit for that department every day. Once you notice problems with heavy shipping days, you will train secondary people to assist when necessary to expedite loads when traffic is heavy.

6. **How long to respond and quote a customer?** How long does it take to get a quote from your

inside sales staff in front of the customer? How long would you wait before you go somewhere else? How long should it take? It may depend upon the complexity of the request. Regardless of your specific issues for your firm, publish a stated internal company goal such as these examples: All quotes out in four hours, one business day, five business days, all quotes with firm pricing good for seven days, all written quotes with firm pricing good for thirty days, etc. You pick the standard and then go with it. You will not achieve it every day because you will find acceptable exceptions and you will build those into your model written on your company policy posted on the wall. Choose a turnaround time for responding to customers, tell the world this policy and then proceed to measure yourself. Once you start this self-evaluation process, you can only get better. Customers will appreciate the fact you have considered this and are working to achieve better faster results for them, even if you are slightly late in the process.

7. **How long to answer potential customer inquiries? (i.e. Calls, emails, text-messages)** How long does it take you to get back with customers? If someone calls your firm and leaves a message with your voicemail, your secretary, your manager, your assistant manager, how long should one wait for a return call? Does it matter if the caller wants to place a $50,000 sales order?

8. **How long to perform a service call for a customer?** How long does it take to get a service man to your home or facility? Does your firm give a promise time, time frame, and time estimate? Do they stick with the plan and if not, do they notify the customer before that time frame lapses?

9. **How long to respond to employee suggestions?** How long does it take for the company to respond to employee suggestions or ideas? Does your company even acknowledge the submission? Does your company respond or tell the employee the idea was received and is being evaluated? Is the employee thanked or recognized for his or her time for the feedback regardless of its importance? Remember that not responding at all is actually destructive to the entire process of encouraging participation so, if your firm does not have the time to respond to ideas or suggestions, do not ask for them.

10. **How long to respond to company website inquiries?** How long does it take for someone to get back with you when you send an inquiry through the internet? Obviously, the longer it takes, the more likely that visitor will never visit again. Do you know from any studies how long it requires to lose a customer for good? The risk of not getting back with him is that he probably will remember very clearly the very poor response and tell a number of people who in turn will further ruin your credibility in the

marketplace. If you cannot respond to website inquiries quickly, do not offer that option.

11. **How long to greet visitors in the company's lobby?** How long does someone wait in the lobby or at your front door waiting for someone to respond, say, "Hello, May I help you?" Even if the receptionist greets the person and announces the visitor to an internal employee, do they have to wait very long for that meeting? Does someone get back with them to let them know they have not been forgotten? Is someone courteous to them?

12. **How long to get a refund from your company?** How long does it take for a customer to get a refund? How long to get it in cash? Credit card? Cashier's check? Is the refund policy posted up at customer service or written on your invoices or receipt?

13. **How long to enter customer sales orders?** How long does it take for a new order to be processed? How long do you think it should take in order for your business to stay competitive?

14. **How long to process customer payments/checks/cash?** How long does it require for your cash application clerk to apply cash? Same day received? Two days? Are your customers complaining? Does the collection person making calls find most of the payments were already sent a week or two ago? If this is the case, why has that person not

spoken up and questioned the timely application of payments?

15. **How long to find "Contact Us" or your telephone number on the company website?** Once a visitor logs onto to your website, how long does it take to figure out how to call your company? If a visitor cannot readily find your telephone number on your website, you should fire your programmer. When visiting your website for the first time, anyone should find a telephone number or "Contact Us" within a few seconds; otherwise, someone is being overpaid. When website visitors cannot figure out how to talk to you, they do not come back.

16. **How long to load up the company website homepage?** How long should it take to load up the front page of your website? Have you had any problems conveyed to you by your customers? Have you had people test it for you to give you feedback? Have you asked? Did you wonder why you do not get many visitors? Can it load up on desktop computers, but not mobile phones? Have you had it tested?

17. **How long to change screens on the company website?** Once one has reached your website, how long does it take to go to another screen? If this fails, the visitor will not wait; he will be like most of us and will leave quickly.

18. **How long to correct wrong employee payroll checks?** How long should I wait if I am employee and you did not pay me for all of my worked time last week? What is the policy?

How long should I have to wait? How am I treated when I work at your facility? If you do not treat me fairly, do you think I may be more likely to overlook problems, steal product or steal time? Do you think if you do not pay me fairly that I will be loyal to your firm?

19. **How long to respond to customer complaints**? How long does it take to get a response back from your firm when your product or service has failed? If your firm fails at this, do you think the buyer will return the next time?

20. **How long before one is greeted with a smile and offered assistance in your facilities?** How long do I have to be in your store before I get someone to greet me or offer me help?

21. **How long after month end are financial statements issued?** How long should management wait in order to get financial statements from your accounting department? How relevant are they if it requires months versus a few days? How likely is it I will be able to increase my borrowing with my bank if I am consistently late with financial statements? How motivated are the managers on incentive programs if they have to wait months before finding out how much they earned for the month? How much of a motivation is it not to know if the company is profitable or not?

22. **How long to ship a customer order?** How long after I order something do you ship it to me? Is it the same day? Is it the same week or

within the month? How long will I be in business if this is not taken critically?

23. **How long to investigate shipment status and locations?** How long does it take for an employee to locate your shipment when you call a company? If it is due soon are they able to give you an answer while you wait on the telephone? If not, you are more likely than not to reconsider using this company again.

24. **How long to wait in the company lobby?** How long do you have to wait in the lobby to speak with someone? The longer you wait, the more you wonder who is at fault here and who simply follows directions. Your concept of this firm diminishes as time passes in the lobby.

25. **How long to pay earned incentives?** How long do your sales people have to wait to get paid incentives or bonuses earned for the benefit of the company? The longer they wait, the less they are likely to wait over the long run and the less they are motivated to do their best for the company. If they have brought new lucrative business to your firm, you need to reward that desired behavior as quickly as possible. Try to pay bonuses monthly or even weekly or semi-monthly if possible. Even though bonuses may be smaller when paid more frequently, sales personnel become rejuvenated when after slow periods new program time frames begin. If they screw up the current month for example, encourage them to get started right away for the next program for the following month.

26. **How long to notice a material decline in new sales orders?** How long does it take to notice new sales orders are drying up? The only way to know this is by measuring actual performance against an established sales forecast previously determined and stated by those responsible for procuring those orders.

27. **How long to notice a lag in collection of outstanding customer receivables?** How long does to take to notice nonpayment by a regularly paying customer? If collection efforts are ongoing and weekly review of the aging occurs, this nonpayment status should be known quickly.

Measure critical tasks and the people who perform them. All of these examples if measured show how well a company is run or how badly it may be neglected. Establishing time limits for each of these important things and putting those quantitative answers into job descriptions and posting them on the wall for the group to see helps to speed things up.

Get your department to establish time limits to increase productivity. No one wants to be the guy who caused a goal to fail. No one wants to be remembered as *'that guy who screwed up the forecast'*. Make decisions and force these departments to declare their turnaround times upfront and hold them to it. Your firm will become more competitive and will generate happier customers. This leads to higher sales, reduced costs and higher profits and that is not a bad idea.

12 Questions To Ask Supervisors About What Training They Feel They Need

Questions to ask any group of supervisors about their experience and need of training:

1. As a supervisor, had you had any experience before this job supervising employees? Were you nervous or worried before you accepted this position, knowing you would be responsible for others reporting to you?

2. Do you think the supervisors that you know well need some type of formalized company training?

3. Are you aware of any supervisor that you privately feel puts the company at risk from a legal standpoint? If you do, why do you feel this way?

4. Have you witnessed anything out of a supervisor that should have been a terminating offense for that individual? If kept confidential, would you state what it was? If not, would you at least describe the offense that you witnessed? If you describe the event you saw, the company can attempt to do some training about it.

5. What type of training do you think the company supervisors should receive?

6. What areas of the company's policies and procedures do you think our supervisors need improvement training?

7. About which part of the supervisors' dealings day to day with numerous subordinates do you think they need some training or good procedural advice?

8. If offered training, what areas of supervision problems would you want covered the most? What type of training do you feel you need the most? Why?

9. As a supervisor, do you have problems in general with terminating employees? If you have not had any in the past, would you like formalized company training for this action required of a supervisor?

10. Do you think most managers need supervisory training or training for supervising subordinates?

11. Do you wish you could be a more effective supervisor? What areas do you want to personally improve?

12. As a supervisor observing other supervisors, what is the one thing that you see lacking in other supervisors in the company that could be helped with formalized training?

12 Reasons To Keep QC Rejected Products From Production To Be Used For Training

Do not throw away rejected products. Retain samples showing problems and use your rejects to your advantage as a good visual training tool.

1. **Take pictures**. Photograph all errors and bad parts and catalog them for future use and training. They document what was wrong with rejected parts. They prove that the company was in error and sometimes, prove the rejection was in error.

2. **Keep examples of all types of rejects**. Do not throw away rejects; these are expensive mistakes that can teach others bad from good parts.

3. **Use bad part examples for training**. Use rejected parts for training new operators on how to lose customers. Show your employees so they can see the difference between good and bad parts. To ensure they are listening, test them.

4. **Display bad parts openly**. If possible, hang bad parts on the wall for all to see and recognize as they pass each day. Post pictures of bad parts so everyone knows and recognizes flaws and which parts not to accept.

5. **Train all employees to recognize bad parts**. Get everyone trained and test them in order to spot mistakes so they can help get them out of your system. Make sure to do this on new parts or new customers.

6. **Who made them?** Trace the bad parts back to the operator and retrain that person until he is flawless at parts production.

7. **Assign only responsible production personnel.** Make it very clear to the employee if he cannot be trained or shows no interest in improving, he must go and be replaced with someone competent who will not threaten the jobs of other employees. You cannot afford to keep bad employees.

8. **Test employees between photos of 'good' and 'bad' parts.** Display them or hang them on the wall along with passing acceptable parts if they both are small. Display them under a sign asking, *"Can you tell which is the good part and which is the bad part?"* or whatever you want as instructive labels.

9. **Reward the best 'producers'. Make perfect parts payoff.** Start this as a contest and give awards to those who demonstrate the best ability at spotting problem parts. Paying your employees is cheaper than paying for rejects and the ultimate loss of a high margin customer.

10. **Your mission is to stop rejects at the door.** You will have rejects but your primary mission is to keep them from ever getting in front of your customers.

11. **Do not hide problems;** show them to all. Don't throw away excellent training examples. Allow all of your employees the ability to observe and study bad parts. Use all production rejects or discovered vendor flaws to train your employees. Do not throw

away this display of company waste. Line them up on the wall or post them up with clear labeling describing the problems on tables in heavy traffic areas of your workers. These errors pose excellent opportunities for instruction.

12. **Your goal is to get new business <u>and</u> keep it**.
    Your first goal is to get new business. Your next goal is make the products your customers want and not to ruin this opportunity. Your employees will make mistakes so as quickly as you can, teach them what not to do. Your most important mission is to keep bad parts from ever getting to a customer so make this the responsibility of everyone who works for your firm.

26 Questions To Ask Machine Operators To Improve Their Productivity And The Company's Profitability

Questions to ask machine operators. Some of these do not directly affect the machine operators but they are in the production plant all day and see problems around them easily fixed if they were in charge.

Here are some typical questions to get started. If you ask, most will be glad to tell you.

1. What machine in your opinion seems to have the most problems or needs to be repaired so we could reduce down time? *Note: You may have to ask this more than once because of being ignored in the past.*

2. Is there a piece of equipment still used in production that everyone knows has problems but is difficult to fix? Which machine is it? Does it cause specific problems in the manufacturing process? Does it require a longer time to make anything?

3. Are there any machines that you think are particularly dangerous to operate? Why do you say this? Have you been instructed not to talk about this risk to employee health?

4. Do you know a machine or piece of equipment that repeatedly has problems that costs the company because of ruined product, increased scrap, slow speed or possibly delayed response? Who in charge has been told about this particular piece of equipment?

5. Which machine ruins or causes the most problems during the manufacturing process? Do you think it is the machine itself or the lack of operator training?

6. What causes unloading incoming trucks to be delayed?

7. What causes delays in quality control?

8. Which jobs are the easiest, fastest jobs to complete that result in no QC problems? (what industry, what's the customer's SIC code to find others like this job)

9. Which jobs cause you, the machine operator, the most headache and are the most difficult to make? (these jobs may need a price hike, or possibly turn them down given opportunity costs to do other easier jobs)

10. What causes delays in customer service?

11. What causes delays at the front desk of your business?

12. What is the one thing that angers your customers more than anything?

13. What is one thing that could be changed to make checking out more pleasant? Or easier? Or faster? Or more fun?

14. Can we make five of something in a row, then cut or separate them simultaneously in the last operation? Versus making one in a row?

15. Are there problems with tooling that need to be corrected or improved? Which product? How does

the tooling negatively impact the time for the production process?

16. What delays you from doing your job that could be corrected, sped up, eliminated, changed or modified in some manner?

17. What do you have to wait on every day that keeps you from starting to work? Is it a person who is too slow, a forklift that will not start, the guard who arrives late who opens the facility door or is it a department where excess absenteeism drives down productivity in all directions?

18. Is there someone or a department that immediately pops into your head that you believe holds up everyone from getting to work and or doing their job because of their inaction, slow response or unpreparedness?

19. I would like for you in the engineering department to devise a method that produces twice as many (you name the product) in the same time that is required now. Remember that even if you do not cut the time in half, any improvement is a great cost savings for the firm.

20. Can we take another look at the current production approach and think about simultaneously making multiple parts versus the current 'one at a time'.

21. Can our tooling be changed in order to make the process faster, easier, on specification, etc.?

22. Can the work center be redesigned (i.e. to be easier, to be faster, to be safer, to be cooler, hotter, to be more efficient, to waste less material)?

23. Do we have the wrong personnel on any work center and if so, what needs to be done to improve profitability? What type of training needs to be done?

24. Do we need to consider paying out an incentive based upon good finished pieces for the work area personnel to boost production?

25. If we need to pay incentives, is there a great firm in town who knows how to do this if we can hire them for this project?

26. If there is someone on staff who knows how to implement a bonus program that will boost production - I need that person to work quickly on this project from start to production finish to ensure we increase our productivity. <u>There is a bonus in it for that guy so find him, **now**</u>!

13 Questions To Ask Your Engineers To Save Costs And Broaden The Product Mix

Try some or all of these questions to ask your engineers about changing products, reducing manufacturing time, using cheaper, different material or eliminating design flaws.

1. What would you change about this product to cut down manufacturing time?

2. Given you are assigned to cut cost and assuming you could change the material on this product, what material would you use instead, and what are your reasons?

3. Being an engineer, what design flaws do you detect in the manufacture of this product? *(Note: Your firm may make products for outside customers and you could offer cost-cutting ideas from your internal engineering group, if that were relevant or if that held a perceived value to your customer group.)*

4. How could we make this product better, combine its manufacture with another piece, combine two pieces into one, manufacture more than one at a time, change material specs to cut cost or add fewer features and patent them, and increase the value of this product?

5. What material in the specification needs to be re-evaluated and possibly substituted in part or whole?

6. How do we take costs out of this product (i.e. material, packaging, process steps, unnecessary finishing, etc.)?

7. What part of the product is overbuilt or overdesigned for the function it provides? Look at overpriced material specifications, overpriced finishes where less is adequate or possibly misses additional uses for this product not yet considered.

8. What on this product is wasted and not necessary?

9. What processes take the longest time or require the greatest amount of labor and differing steps?

10. What can be dropped, cut off, trimmed, reduced, cut back or changed to eliminate process steps?

11. Does the product do what it is supposed to do or is it overdesigned, poorly designed, designed incorrectly or awkwardly?

12. Which jobs should we avoid given our current machines?

13. What machines should we be buying given our opportunities with new customers? And will those new machines require employee training or newhires with expertise?

14 Items To Consider Including On Your Company Credit Reference Report

Your firm is asked to complete credit applications and write down vendors who will vouch for your ability to pay. If you put together a standard credit reference report, this cuts down the time to complete those applications. Consider including these items in your company's credit reference report.

1. Company: name, address and other major facility addresses (offices and warehouses)

2. Product descriptions: Give a very brief description of what your firm sells, provides. (i.e. Canada's largest yogurt manufacturer, premium real and look-a-like leather goods, importer of choice oriental perfumes and scents, heavy metal manufacturing of bronze, copper, silver, gold and other various alloys, variety of metal plating services, distributor of over $100M worth of brands of personal hygiene care products, professional dance lessons for customers up to 16 years old, classic piano lessons for over 39 years)

3. Physical addresses, remit addresses, warehouse ship to addresses

4. Company telephone, main email address and any fax numbers

5. Company owners' names, titles (do not give home addresses), indicate that the owners will or will not sign personal guarantees

6. Accounts Payable contact information; name, telephone, fax and AP email address for invoice submissions.

7. Bank(s) addresses, loan officers, telephone and fax numbers and email addresses, mention lines of credit that are open and who to call to verify business loans and credit (do not make the vendor have to ask for this because they must have your permission ---make it easy for them)

8. Credit references; the more the better - (list name, address, telephone numbers and contact names and titles) for at least seven to ten or more vendors of substantial size who you know ahead of time will give good or excellent credit references if independently contacted

9. Federal identification number (EIN)

10. Dun and Bradstreet number (if applicable)

11. SIC industry code(s) served

12. If you are public, give the trading symbol for your company and stock exchange,

13. If you are private, you may or may not mention audited financial statements are available if necessary (all dependent upon the magnitude of the contemplated purchase).

14. Include a few of your advertisement flyers showing what you manufacture, sell, distribute or service.

29 Possible Questions To Ask Your CPA Firm To Compare Your Performance To Others In The Industry

Your CPA firm does hundreds of external required CPA financial YE audits each year so there is a good chance they may audit other similar businesses such as your own. It would help your management to ask your CPA firm if they would compare your financial performance to others in the same industry but without names (i.e. financial ratios concerning debt, profitability, debt and liquidity ratios, cash flow, bank interest rates).

Questions to ask your CPA firm (statistics, organization type, financial performance, etc.):

1. How well does our company do financially, compared to other players participating in the same market segment? Where does our net profit % compare? Where does our return on assets compare? Where does our return on investment compare?

2. How does our company's heads per sales dollar figure compared to others competing in our market?

3. What do you see about our firm that is out of line, more costly, less efficient or obviously ineffective compared to others that you privately audited and personally know?

4. Is our firm's headcount in line with the industry? (Compare annual sales per head if that seems appropriate.) Is our people count higher or lower given our current sales level? Even if our overall headcount may be line with industry standards,

what about the internal department or function numbers; headcount in sales, production or administration?

5. Given our number of facilities, does the average sales per facility seem correct, low or high compared to others?

6. Do we generate about the same, higher or lower gross profit per operational unit (location) as others in our market?

7. If we are lower on average concerning profit per facility, does it make sense for our firm to consider combining facilities in order to cut fixed costs and maximize gross profit generated per profit center?

8. Are our sales and marketing expenses as a percentage of net sales in line with our business segment compared to other clients?

9. Do we have healthy gross profit margins compared to others in our business? Are we higher or lower? If we are significantly different, where do you see the variance?

10. How does our administrative expense percentage of net sales compare to others in the market?

11. Are our insurance costs in line with the market segment?

12. Is our property tax bill high or low or just about right compared to the industry? (i.e. tax bill as a percentage of depreciated net book value? Or historical cost? Or appraised value?)

13. What are the average annual capital expenditures for other competitors in our market? Are we spending more or less than the average?

14. What geographical markets are our company missing compared to the competitors? Where should we be if we are not?

15. What do you see that is obviously different when you enter our facility and when you enter that facility of our competitor?

16. Do we generate adequate cost data compared to other players in our market?

17. Do we use our cost data to our advantage or are we missing any key statistics that should be tracked on a regular basis?

18. Did you notice anything out of line concerning the company's pricing? Too many cheap items? Too many expensive options?

19. Is there a part of the market that we have missed?

20. Is there a part of the market that we should either change our marketing or consider abandoning?

21. Do we need to shop for a better loan rates from what you have seen in the market?

22. If your other clients are in the loan market and getting better interest rates than us, what are those notes? How unfavorable are we from your other clients?

23. Are you aware of better banks or financial institutions that we should speak with to obtain favorable financing?

24. Is our insurance cost in line with others in the industry? Are deductibles too high or too low? Is coverage adequate to cover the owners?

25. Did you receive any negative comments from customers when you personally verified accounts receivable balances at yearend? Were there any complaints or comments about our quality?

26. Is our electricity cost per kilowatt higher or lower than the others that the auditor shares as clients? Can the auditor get this information without company names in order to get some idea if utility costs are competitive or not? Auditing hundreds of clients should yield an opportunity.

27. Does our company have any unclaimed property in this or any other state?

28. What is our property tax as a percentage of net sales compared to others? If that is not a good financial measurement, what is a better one?

29. How do we fare concerning labor benefits compared to others in our industry? (i.e. better or worse insurance life insurance, a 401K match, pension program).

20 Steps To File State Unclaimed Property Claims For Your Company And Yourself

Every state in the U.S. has unclaimed property funds as old as 25 to 30 years sent in by a variety of vendors. If your company has ever had an office or warehouse in a state, you should assign someone on your staff to look into those states' funds every year because funds are being added by law every year, all without any accumulating interest.

Here are some simple instructions to follow to get started for your company as well as for yourself and family.

1. Google or search your state name and the words "unclaimed property". For example, in Indiana, search "Indiana Unclaimed Property" or in Texas, type in the search bar, "Texas Unclaimed Property".

2. Click on that state website that holds a search engine.

3. Find the search button on the website and enter your company's name.

4. Vary the spelling for common misspellings to ensure the check is not held under a slightly different name.

5. Some of the states allow you to search by street so try this also (i.e. previous addresses for warehouses, offices, previously owned businesses).

6. Search diligently. Try numerous spellings. A company named "The Cleaning Company" may

be listed under "the", "cleaning" or maybe "company". Try all variations.

7. Some search engines will find too many or maybe not disclose who sent in the money so you must practice searching to get an understanding how the state's search engine works.

8. Be sure to search unclaimed property for your individual name as well as the business name.

9. Be sure to search unclaimed property in each state where your company has or had physical offices even if those properties are no longer owned. The funds held by these states have monies back to the 1990s.

10. Be sure to search for unclaimed property for you in each state where you have lived, rented or owned residences or properties personally.

11. Search with as few letters as possible to find the name of relatives. (i.e. Jo...smith for Joseph Smith or if possible, look through all of the Smiths listed.)

12. Try not to limit the search by entering a city since you do not know how they may have entered the returned funds to the state.

13. Try individuals' last names first without a first name, then add the first letter of the first name until you begin to receive results.

14. Search for all previous maiden names.

15. Search deceased people; estate representatives or legal heirs will have to claim these funds.

16. Search common misspellings because many of these entries were hand typed into the system years ago.

17. Review all similar names that do not have addresses or towns listed in the results. Look for recognizable sources such as your bank or ex-bank, your credit union or ex-credit union, an old 401K fiduciary institution, apartment complex or real estate company where you might have lived for a potential missed deposit, a familiar utility company name where you may have left a deposit.

18. Search non-profits for last donations.

19. When you file your claims, put copies of business cards, drivers' licenses, corporate tax return filings (front page) to identify who you are to be filed along with the state claim form. If the check sent to the state was a refund from a prior vendor, include a copy of some of your prior purchases during this time to prove your firm had dealings with this vendor. It will help your case.

20. File your claims, make copies to keep as backup, prior to mailing and follow up over the next few months (states are slow to pay).

34 Financial Measurements To Consider Tracking For Your Company

Here are a few assorted measurements that are used by many companies to track financial and productive performance. Too many companies do not calculate them and the ones that do publish the results too late for management to react. Many of these calculations should be reviewed regularly. Most should be viewed on a historic perspective. Some should be measured monthly or weekly. Some should be tallied every day.

1. **Net sales** (per month, year, region, salesman, product type, service type)

2. **Gross profit dollars** or gross profit **percentages** by product line, profit center and or by week, month, QTD and YTD.

3. **Net profit** (per month, year, region, salesman, product type, service type). Do you know if you are better or worse than your competitors doing the same thing? Find out.

4. **Number of tests performed** (laboratory analyses) for measuring productivity (possibly divided by headcount).

5. **Dollars credited back to customers** (sorted by rejects, bad parts, too many parts shipped, parts shipped too late, etc.) You want to know how much is given away and how easily that is happening.

6. **Number and dollar amount of invoices billed** per day, week, month (or average dollar amount per invoice or shipment). This works well visually on a chart accompanied by a trendline.

7. **Number of indirect people versus direct people** (the lower the better for production in

manufacturing). This will change as you buy automated equipment so adjust your expectations for the measurement number.

8. **Number of quotes won versus total quoted** (100% won means your prices quoted are too low whereas 0% won means prices quoted are too high). Quotes won does not mean they are profitable. For the ones you have one, what was their return?

9. **Sales orders** received sorted by salesman, then sorted highest sales orders received to lowest dollar amount received (watch the bottom of the list for cutting or raising prices).

10. **Most profitable jobs**, projects, products or services Watch these because at some point you may need to exit a market and enter another. Sort your sales by SIC code, industry, etc. to find the more profitable group of companies that are available for a reasonable amount of cost.

11. **Least profitable jobs**, projects, products or services. Is this a particular group of customers or an industrial group or maybe they are in a crowded market where margins are slim and there are too many hungry competitors.

12. Customers with the **lowest net profit %**s. You will need to evaluate this group and slowly raise prices and let the customers decide.

13. Customers with the **highest net profit %s.** Watch this group to make sure they are happy and contented, otherwise this does not last long once competitors smell the available money.

14. **Number of items rejected** versus total produced from various production machines. You might record this ratio at various speeds on the machine if the operator can control production speed. Watch

machines and continue to run paybacks for the purchase of newer faster or more accurate equipment.

15. **Dollars taken on early payment discounts** (percent discounts offered by vendors if you pay their invoices earlier than previously negotiated per the terms on their invoice)

16. **Sales dollars per number of heads** ((monthly sales X 12)/ number of equivalent fulltime people) possibly compared to recorded industry standards.

17. **Total value of purchase orders** placed for the month. (Listing of highest to lowest vendors from this list should provide target companies for purchasing to attempt to renegotiate prices.)

18. **Overtime dollars and hours** compared to straight earned wages, overtime converted to equivalent heads (this premium paid generates no additional sales and acts as a penalty). There is a breakeven point where it does not make sense to hire if the situation is temporary, but if not, it is time to hire some people and cut back the premium dollars hemorrhaging on your P&L.

19. **Salary increases** as a percentage of total base pay. Does it seem reasonable for your market and industry?

20. **Sales commissions** as a percentage of base pay for incentivized personnel (i.e. salespeople).

21. **Freight costs** as a percentage of sales to consider alternative delivery options.

22. Track the **costs of the top ten cost items offered or used by a restaurant**. (i.e. steak costs, lobster costs, prime rib costs, port wine costs, caviar costs, etc.). Someone should be doing this simply so the

restaurant can adjust pricing to market rates in their printed menus in order to maintain margins.

23. Track and post the average of the top five or six **mortgage rates offered by the local banks** for home buyers to see as they enter your office.

24. Count and track **incoming sales order**s by week by salesperson, if not tracked now. Post the graph on the wall versus a budget, higher or lower?

25. For retail companies, count the **number of customers** per day through your front door. Chart the number by day of week and time of month. Measure the count against sales dollars. (i.e. 200 people in, 164 purchases, 36 people who did not find anything they wished to buy. Why did they decide not to buy?)

26. Keep a chart of total **number of invoices**, total **number of shipments**, average sales dollars per shipment, as measured a year ago for the same month, quarter to date, year to date.

27. In appropriate industries where the market can be reasonably estimated, gather best guesses from all of the sales personnel as to how much of the customer's business your firm currently has (% of estimated total purchases for that service or product from each customer). Once these customer totals are tallied, the company can estimate how large the market is and what piece the company currently shares. This **approximation of market shar**e helps upper management decide how many more people to hire, where to hire, what to manufacture or sell and what capital in which to invest. It also assists with outside lending and getting sources of capital for the company's future growth.

28. **Customers complaints** and the ultimate resolutions to those complaints categorized by type (measured against history reflecting either improvement, worsening; all resulting in a better understanding of sales problems).

29. **Average age of capital** in use (age analysis of pieces of machinery)

30. **Maintenance and repair costs** as a percentage of net sales or percentage of total costs.

31. **Top vendor purchases**

32. **Top customer sales**

33. **Analysis of all freight costs** categorized by type (customer deliveries, product pickup and delivery, expediting fees for late shipments,etc.)

34. **Categorization of Services or Products** by process, function or some other applicable sorting denominator. (i.e. products sales and gross profit dollars originally made on $1.2M piece of equipment versus those products made on a $ 50,000 piece of equipment).

6 Steps To Take Before And 11 Steps To Take After Company Vehicle Accidents

All of your company drivers need to be instructed on what precautions they must take and what to do before they drive the company car, truck, van or other vehicle. When they indeed are involved in an accident in the future, make sure to have a checklist prepared for them sitting in the dashboard ready to be read.

Checklist of actions to take prior to accidents:

1. Before any accident occurs, ensure the current insurance card for that vehicle is kept in the assigned glove compartment of the correct car.

2. Give renewal cards to the drivers before the expiration date occurs.

3. Ask the drivers to bring the insurance cards into the office as a check or ask they send a picture of them to the office periodically to ensure they are in compliance and have the current cards in the vehicle with them.

4. If your company has the cards online or stored in the company telephones, require that the drivers demonstrate that they know where they are and can show them to an officer upon request from their assigned telephones.

5. Ensure your office has a spare key to the vehicle at all times.

6. Review the following accident checklist with each assigned driver.

Checklist of actions to take after an accident occurs:

1. Call an ambulance first for anyone injured. (most locations, use '911')

2. Call the police and tell them you want them to make a report.

3. Write down the other vehicle's license plate number before anything. (In case they take off and do not offer their information. If this happens, call the police as you normally would.)

4. Do not leave the scene of the accident.

5. Do not move cars unless people are in danger (on a speeding highway, near a dangerous cliff, etc.).

6. Take pictures of the accident showing damage, license plate numbers, other drivers, witnesses.

7. Write down names and telephone numbers of any witnesses and all involved in the accident.

8. Do not discuss the accident with the other driver or drivers.

9. Obtain the accident report from the reporting officer. He may give you an assigned number. The official report will occur later that day or afterwards.

10. Get the name, address, phone number, driver's license number, insurance company, policy number and insurance company telephone number of the other driver.

11. Write down the exact time and date of the accident.

12. Write down and describe the exact location of the accident (clear physical address). Draw a map if you must.

13. Note the weather and road conditions (stop light not working, ongoing construction, one way street, exits blocked, raining, sleet, snowing, blizzard, tornado?).

16 Questions To Ask Before You Buy A Foreign Insurance Policy

Before your firm buys a foreign insurance policy to cover your company assets outside of the U.S., find out what the policy will NOT pay and what to do in a number of circumstances.

Here are some questions to ask before buying these foreign insurance policies.

1. Do you need us to notify the insurance company that we are going out of the country before we leave on the trip? And mention what we intend to do there?

2. Can our employees rent cars and trucks to drive in that country?

3. Must we specify ahead of time to our insurance company the countries where we wish to conduct business?

4. What is the list of countries not covered by insurance?

5. If our employees are caught and arrested with illegal substances, banned items or any other type of contraband specific in that country, are any of these costs covered by the policy or are they on their own?

6. If we hire a trucking firm to move freight for us and the load disappears and is not covered by this foreign freight firm, does this insurance policy cover any of these losses? If it does, what are the

restrictions? If it does not, what type of policy do we need to purchase?

7. If our employees have an accident, what must they do? When do they report it to our insurance company? What type of damage is covered? What is not covered? What is the deductible?

8. If the policy is for $1M and the employee does more damage than this limit, can the balance of the claim revert to an existing excess or umbrella coverage policy, or are there restrictions?

9. We want company owned machinery, raw material, work in process and all finished goods that are sitting in a foreign country to be covered for fire, theft and other accidents. What types of losses are not covered in this policy?

10. If our employees take their spouses or family members and they are hurt, does this policy pay for their injury? If this policy does not cover these losses, what type of policy should the employee purchase himself?

11. If our employees drink, drive and kill someone in the foreign country, does the insurance policy cover this?

12. Do we need to specify all of the employees' names who will be driving company vehicles before the coverage starts?

13. If the employee rents a car and does damage to the car, does this company policy cover that? If it does

not, how do we get auto coverage for our employees?

14. Does this policy cover any type of ransom or costs if our employees or visiting staff are kidnapped? If so, what are the limits and what are the types of circumstances covered?

15. Are the countries that are covered in our company's policy recommended for driving? If not, is there a list of countries not covered for private employee driving?

16. If we go to the foreign warehouse that we were using and everything is cleaned out and everyone is gone, how do we report this loss to the insurance company? How does this type of loss claim work? What are the steps to document this financial claim?

15 Basic Ideas To Cut Any Company's Commercial Insurance Premium Cost

Here are a few ideas for a business to implement that should drive the annual insurance costs down. Thus, try these ways to actively cut and reduce your commercial insurance costs:

1. Classify your employees into the correct workman's compensation code to minimize your premium (based upon gross payroll for most employees). There are over 600 possible codes so misclassifying employees has a large monetary impact on your calculated premium. Look them up.

2. Emphasize employee safety programs.

3. Train employees and terminate those who ignore company safety rules.

4. Reward those employees with excellent safety records. Make it payoff economically for all employees to be and operate proactively safe in your company.

5. Include safety and no accidents as bonus criteria.

6. Buy vehicles that carry cheaper insurance costs. These are easier to repair, have fewer accidents and are cheaper to replace.

7. Pay your premiums quarterly or semi-monthly versus monthly and get a discount.

If it makes economic sense, increase the policies' deductibles when the company can financially afford to chip in on accidents. It makes lots of sense when your company has very few or no accidents.

8. The better the credit history your company has, the lower the cost premium will be.

9. Bundle policies together with your insurance agent where possible (general liability (GL) and property insurance).

10. Ask your agent to give you options to cut your insurance premium costs. That is part of his job so ask him.

11. Manage your internal risks by having an active safety training program.

12. Invite your insurance company to come and audit (for free) your facilities and follow their recommendations. It will pay off at premium time.

13. Manage your internal risks by installing an effective security system.

14. Teach employee how to religiously set alarms before leaving and locking up the premises.

15. Manage your risks by having written, well established, job procedures to minimize hazards.

32 Suggestions For Intern Assignments To Boost Productivity And Save Your Company Money

Hire an intern specifically to complete assigned projects. Here is a list that your firm might consider that college-age intern candidates should be able to do which will help your firm and save money.

1. **Inventory equipment list and location map:** Inventory all company equipment noting make, model, year built, serial number and any other pertinent data about each piece. Draw a layout to locate each within the company facilities. Note 800 service numbers or contact information on these machines. Open them up and search for other information to note unique for the machine.

2. **Equipment critical parts/where to get them:** Research and document vital equipment parts by machine. Note telephone and vendor service names and contact information and post on each applicable machine in protected plastic sleeves for easy reference in case of breakdown. This will allow faster notice for service in the case of downtimes. If you prefer, assemble a manual easily referenced and regularly updated to be used by maintenance and service personnel.

3. **Post critical part information on each machine:** Research all critical part numbers for each piece of machinery and post with the machine with telephone numbers, service numbers, etc.

4. **Fixed assets tagged with plant grid layout:** Inventory all company assets and tag each item.

Create plant grid layout in order to locate each item (i.e. Building A: aisle #1, machine location 3, aisle #4, machine location 11).

5. **Asset loans tied to bank loans (open balances):** Tie all company assets back to bank loan numbers and amounts in order to know immediately when items have open balances.

6. **Lost sales from unused machines:** Track all unused machine time and convert it into lost absorption or lost sales. Track, report and post this every day to put pressure on sales to fill up your machinery. (i.e. plant production = 87% of full capacity or $40K of lost sales per day).

7. **Use SIC Codes from current customers to find new sales:** Research new potential customers by tracking the SIC codes of your current customers. The same or similar SIC codes may point to more sales possibilities and all of this data can be obtained online free with a library card.

8. **New programs assignment:** Research the viability of a new program, campaign, or initiative; compile and present statistics.

9. **Troublesome projects:** Complete a backburner project that has been bogging down permanent staff.

10. **Social media campaigns:** Create a proposal on a potential social media strategy, evaluate various social media platforms, or come up with suggestions for how your current social media strategy might be improved.

11. **Website critiques (pros/cons):** Critique your company's website from a user perspective; gather ideas from outside observers, track complaints and brainstorm ideas for boosting usability.

12. **Website usefulness (what is missing?):** Poll customers on usefulness of company website and gather suggestions as to desirable changes that can be made or altered to make the site more useful.

13. **Industry blogs and issue relevant news weekly report:** Research, identify and follow the most influential blogs in your industry. Follow them and provide weekly reports of the best ideas, innovations, new equipment, new products introduced within your company's industry.

14. **News articles and developments:** Scan industry media for news items; provide regularly scheduled updates.

15. **Observe sales meetings/ log decisions, assignments:** Accompany employees to client, sales, or other outside meetings; have them take an observer role, but ask for their input and ideas (and answer any questions) after you've left.

16. **IT evaluation:** Evaluate some area of IT functionality (for tech-savvy interns); ask if they see a way to improve efficiency, streamline programs, or cut costs.

17. **Assign a daily task/duty:** Take responsibility for some regular task. Even if it's as simple as taking, and placing, the weekly supply order, it will demonstrate follow-through and an ability to take

ownership. Calculate and chart daily sales, daily returns, items manufactured, sold or made. Keep track and publish earned incentives, oil, gas, lumber prices, hog futures, new customers, product margins (best to worst), store sales (highest to lowest), best and worst sales personnel, office supply usage or scrap generation or revenue.

18. **Prepare a budget:** It does not have to be the corporate budget. Select a department, source of revenue, particular store or branch or troublesome division to analyze and dissect.

19. **Graphs/visuals:** Create support materials, such as charts, graphs, or other visuals.

20. **Events/meetings:** Plan and coordinate an event or meeting.

21. **Marketing plan:** Generate a marketing plan, financial forecast, or other report. Start with demographics, price points, desirable profit margins, etc.

22. **Videos:** Produce a video or slide presentation.

23. **Customer AP Contacts:** Create a list of all customer personnel who are in charge of paying your company. Get names, telephone numbers, email addresses, physical addresses, fax numbers.

24. **Product studies:** Perform a study or survey; analyze and present results. (i.e. worst profit margin products, slowest selling items, least desirable colors or finishes, worst return rates to customer service, etc.)

25. **Customer polls:** Ask 1,000 customers what they use your product for and document all of these various uses.

26. **Employee manuals:** Compile employee manuals or develop process directions for tasks with high employee turnover. Survey workers to see what is missing or needed for inclusion in the next updated version.

27. **Low cost source alternatives:** Source goods or search for lower-cost sources for high-volume materials. Identify alternative vendors through market research.

28. **Purchasing manual:** Assemble a purchasing manual (database) of all the goods and services purchased. Research all vendors' names, contact names, telephone numbers, fax numbers, email addresses and a 30-50-character text box or comment indicating anything unique about ordering or how to order to gain lowest prices.

29. **Database cleaning:** Clean up a database (customer list, vendors paid, full time employees, accounts payable files, machine, equipment, vehicle or service files, maintenance lists, oil change mile suggestions and due dates and times for in-use company cars and trucks, dates for license plates renewals, amounts, locations and coverage levels for insurance).

30. **AP Liaison:** Serve as a liaison between the company and clients or vendors (freeing up staff

members to communicate on only more crucial issues).

31. **Train new or replacement interns:** Help screen and train replacement interns prior to departure.

32. **Worst products/services:** Have a financial analyst intern investigate the top ten worst performing products and then analyze the companies or buyers to see similarities or common points or features. Do the same for top performing products in order to understand who is buying them and to identify more potential customers.

11 Questions To Ask, Answer and Implement Procedures To Repair "Down" Production Machines

Here are some questions to ask and procedures to establish specifically for your company when machines are down and require maintenance.

1. How long does it take from the moment the machine goes down until maintenance is notified? Ten minutes? Thirty minutes? One hour? Next shift? Next day? Know this average time lapsed immediately.

2. Who is responsible to report machine downtime?

3. At what point does a machine that is down get reported? Is there a time frame or limit? (i.e. within five minutes, by the end of the shift, as soon as the machine is needed).

4. Is the reporting requirement for a down machine listed in the job description of the operator?

5. Is it part of the operator's job description to notify the production supervisor when bad parts are being made? (Sign of machine problems).

6. Is it part of the operator's job description to notify the production supervisor when his assigned machine is making odd irregular noises or when there are problems operating the machine?

7. How quickly are machines repaired? What is expected of the maintenance department?

8. Is there a list of machines out of order which lists all machines down, an estimated town to be fixed and the cost estimate to make the repairs.

9. Do maintenance personnel know to get permission before spending any money on down or broken machines with an age over (you fill in the age) 10 years old? The machine may not be worth the cost when there may be another new model that is faster and can be financed and installed quickly.

10. Are maintenance personnel properly trained on all of the machines by the manufacturers?

11. Are maintenance personnel sent off site to attend training sessions at the manufacturer's facilities?

Make employees responsible for reporting machine problems. If you do not know any of this procedure, ask. Keep probing and you will find gaps. Many times, procedures are written but not taught, nor are they repeated to stress the importance of keeping all machines operating. Make sure the onus is put on the employee because the production supervisor cannot cover all of the departments. He must depend upon good operators.

23 Questions To Ask Your Employees When Your Company Is Losing Money

Start asking some or all of these questions when your firm is heading towards losses.

1. Because we are not profitable at this time, we need everyone's help in cutting costs, raising quality and improving sales. Do you have any ideas now that you would like to offer to boost the bottom line?

2. How can we make more money? Do not worry about your idea not being detailed; in simple terms, what do you think we are doing wrong?

3. Where do you personally (concerning your job or department) see every day that we need to cut costs?

4. Where do we waste the most money? Describe the department, group of people, product involved, position, function, etc.

5. What about the company procedures of taking orders, processing orders, buying materials and supplies, spending labor dollars and shipping product seems to be inefficient to you?

6. What part of the company manufacturing process needs to be evaluated because it is wasteful and takes too long?

7. What is wrong with the company's service? What can be done to improve it and make the customers want to call us again in the future?

8. Why do you think we have rework and rejected parts? Who primarily do you think causes these problems in the company? Who is not doing their job?

9. Where do you see the largest waste of valuable company funds?

10. Do you think there is too much overtime spent by the company? If so, who would you say in what department?

11. Why do you think we have too much overtime?

12. What one thing could the company do to reduce overtime?

13. Do you see waste in the company in labor or spending? If so, where do you see it on a regular basis?

14. If you had to cut costs, what would you cut right now starting today that you feel is hemorrhaging money?

15. What is the second thing that you would cut right now?

16. What would you suggest to in order to increase sales? What group of buyers are we missing?

17. What do you think we need to do to improve customer relations?

18. What machines (cost centers) that you know about need to be serviced and improved in order to cut costs and improve product margins? Tell us the

specific machines and why they do not operate properly. Which need to be replaced?

19. What items are too costly or wasted in the plant?

20. What service performed needs to be brought back in-house?

21. Ok, tomorrow you are in charge and need to cut costs. What is the first thing you would cut or reduce the cost because it is wasteful?

22. What material that we buy gets wasted or generates a lot of questionable scrap? Please provide some examples.

23. Assuming your answer is kept confidential, are you aware of any theft occurring in the company that you feel you want to discuss or disclose?

Offer anonymity if necessary – mail suggestions outside. For those answering questions, offer them the following response option. If you do not feel comfortable about publicly answering the above question about theft or questionable activities among employees, we are posting an outside address of our CPA firm where you can mail an anonymous tip. You may address your tip to "Company Name Tips", c/o of our CPA firm.

Instruct your CPA firm to retain the anonymity of requested when submitting ideas.

14 Required Employee Comments To Be Submitted Before They Clock Out And Leave For The Day

Ask all employees before leaving for home at the end of their shift to see their supervisor and make any appropriate or necessary comments about any of these open issues listed below. Tweak the list as necessary to make it appropriate for your firm's specific needs.

1. Were you able to finish all of your production assignments today? If yes, did you turn in all required production reports?

2. If you did not finish all assignments today, did you report directly (talk, not email or text) what was not finished to your supervisor?

3. Who are you waiting on in order to bill a customer for a shipment? (billings clerk)

4. Were there any irate customer calls today and if so, were they resolved by the appropriate parties (sales department)? If there were and they were not resolved, please let us know the customers' names before leaving. (receptionist)

5. Is there anything wrong you noticed with the machine you operated today? (machinist)

6. Was your assigned machine making more than normal amount of bad parts today? Do you know the reason why, and is it resolved (for the next operator)? (machine operator)

7. Was there anything odd that occurred today? (i.e. lights flickering, power went down, material not

delivered to the machine by shift's end by the material handler, machine electronic display was not working properly). (all employees)

8. The written filed maintenance request is still on the supervisor's desk and remains unassigned several hours after the first incident caused parts failure.

9. Which operators during the last shift are causing the most delays in production?

10. What tooling needs to be fixed on the 2nd shift or else no parts will be run tomorrow?

11. What task or tasks did you not get done by the time you were assigned to leave today? Is it important and can it wait until tomorrow?

12. Before you go, is there any customer we told we would call back but did not call yet?

13. Did all of the mail get taken to the post office?

14. Did all of the overnight envelopes get taken to the appropriate boxes before their deadline for pickups?

26 Questions To Ask Machine Operators To Improve Their Productivity And The Company's Profitability

Questions to ask machine operators. Some of these do not directly affect the machine operators but they are in the production plant all day and see problems around them easily fixed if they were in charge.

Here are some typical questions to get started. If you ask, most will be glad to tell you.

1. What machine in your opinion seems to have the most problems or needs to be repaired so we could reduce down time? *Note: You may have to ask this more than once because of being ignored in the past.*

2. Is there a piece of equipment still used in production that everyone knows has problems but is difficult to fix? Which machine is it? Does it cause specific problems in the manufacturing process? Does it require a longer time to make anything?

3. Are there any machines that you think are particularly dangerous to operate? Why do you say this? Have you been instructed not to talk about this risk to employee health?

4. Do you know a machine or piece of equipment that repeatedly has problems that costs the company because of ruined product, increased scrap, slow speed or possibly delayed response? Who in charge has been told about this particular piece of equipment?

5. Which machine ruins or causes the most problems during the manufacturing process? Do you think it is the machine itself or the lack of operator training?

6. What causes unloading incoming trucks to be delayed?

7. What causes delays in quality control?

8. Which jobs are the easiest, fastest jobs to complete that result in no QC problems? (what industry, what's the customer's SIC code to find others like this job)

9. Which jobs cause you, the machine operator, the most headache and are the most difficult to make? (these jobs may need a price hike, or possibly turn them down given opportunity costs to do other easier jobs)

10. What causes delays in customer service?

11. What causes delays at the front desk of your business?

12. What is the one thing that angers your customers more than anything?

13. What is one thing that could be changed to make checking out more pleasant? Or easier? Or faster? Or more fun?

14. Can we make five of something in a row, then cut or separate them simultaneously in the last operation? Versus making one in a row?

15. Are there problems with tooling that need to be corrected or improved? Which product? How does

the tooling negatively impact the time for the production process?

16. What delays you from doing your job that could be corrected, sped up, eliminated, changed or modified in some manner?

17. What do you have to wait on every day that keeps you from starting to work? Is it a person who is too slow, a forklift that will not start, the guard who arrives late who opens the facility door or is it a department where excess absenteeism drives down productivity in all directions?

18. Is there someone or a department that immediately pops into your head that you believe holds up everyone from getting to work and or doing their job because of their inaction, slow response or unpreparedness?

19. I would like for you in the engineering department to devise a method that produces twice as many (you name the product) in the same time that is required now. Remember that even if you do not cut the time in half, any improvement is a great cost savings for the firm.

20. Can we take another look at the current production approach and think about simultaneously making multiple parts versus the current 'one at a time'.

21. Can our tooling be changed in order to make the process faster, easier, on specification, etc.?

22. Can the work center be redesigned (i.e. to be easier, to be faster, to be safer, to be cooler, hotter, to be more efficient, to waste less material)?

23. Do we have the wrong personnel on any work center and if so, what needs to be done to improve profitability? What type of training needs to be done?

24. Do we need to consider paying out an incentive based upon good finished pieces for the work area personnel to boost production?

25. If we need to pay incentives, is there a great firm in town who knows how to do this if we can hire them for this project?

26. If there is someone on staff who knows how to implement a bonus program that will boost production - I need that person to work quickly on this project from start to production finish to ensure we increase our productivity. There is a bonus in it for that guy so find him, **now**!

Ask Your Employees These 23 Simple Questions Every Week And Discover How To Make More Money

Company employees many times know the answers to the company's problems but have not been asked. Try asking these questions from employees each week. Pick and choose which you think are relevant but make sure to keep the questions open as much as possible. Do not narrow their responses.

Questions to ask your company's employees:

1. What one place, department, machine or function causes the largest waste of company money?

2. Which products does the company make best?

3. Which products does the company fail at producing? Repeatedly?

4. Which company machines do you think are the best, most productive and easiest to operate?

5. Which machines seem to be the most unused? Sitting idle with no operators?

6. Which company machines are the worst to operate, ruin materials, stop unexpectedly, cause production delays or is just difficult to run on a regular basis?

7. Which machines cause the most accidents?

8. Which machines ruin the most products or materials?

9. Which machines are the worst ones or take the longest to fix for the maintenance guys?

10. Which customers products are the most difficult to make or prepare or take the most time?

11. Which products that we make are the easiest, fastest and seem to be the most profitable?

12. Which services that we provide seem to be the worst or most difficult to complete?

13. What tools are we missing that would help the process in the plant proceed more quickly?

14. Where do you see the largest waste of money, if you can name only one? (Ask everyone as well as the maintenance guys. They fix the problems and must spend money quickly.)

15. What would be the next two or three areas of waste you think may be costing too much company money?

16. Which group of employees (department) needs more training, help or assistance? (Ask this question of everyone but especially of the QC personnel who determine rejects.)

17. Which materials that the company buys seems to be ruined, wasted or lost the most? (Ask the material handlers and inventory personnel this question. They see the write-offs.)

18. Which customers are the worst to service or most demanding? (Ask the service department this question as well as your drivers.)

19. Which customers seem to reject shipments the most? (Ask receiving personnel this question.)

20. Which customers call most frequently with complaints? (Ask the receptionist and anyone who

answers incoming calls as well as customer service representatives.)

21. What area of the plant or store does maintenance spend the most time?

22. What type of products have the highest failure rate? (Ask Quality Control as well as other production personnel.)

23. From which machines do the largest number of rejects come? (Ask Quality Control as well as production supervision.)

7 Simple Negotiation Techniques For All Of Your Buyers To Learn

All purchasing agents are different and each has different valuable skills. The best thing a company can do is meet with all of its buyers, accumulate their techniques and then teach the entire group all of the techniques so every buyer is better from the experience. Here are a few basic techniques that will help any buyer purchase more intelligently.

1. **Low Volume/High Volume:** Call a potential vendor, ask for a quote (request for quote, RFQ), give a low volume (100 per month), and negotiate the best price including or excluding delivery and packaging methods. Once you have been told this is the best price adamantly by the vendor, ask for a price for higher volume, (i.e. 1000 per month).

2. **Pricing With/ Without Freight:** Negotiate the best price from a vendor delivered (freight included), then ask for the price if the product is picked up by your own truck.

3. **Pricing With / Without Material:** Negotiate a manufacturing price from a vendor all inclusive (material, delivery, etc.), then ask what the price could be if you purchase the material or perform an outside service. Your firm may buy large volumes of this material already so your current pricing may be lower than that of your new vendor, thus the request for two pricing levels.

4. **Freebies with longer commitment:** Negotiate landscaping maintenance per month with a

minimum number of visits per month, then request flowers and flower bed maintenance be thrown in once per quarter or semi-annually if you sign a quarterly or annual maintenance contract. (i.e. Free items for a longer-term commitment).

5. **Better price on quicker payment:** Negotiate best pricing for low volume, then high volume, then declare you pay vendors in 60 days unless you can get a better price then you can swing 30 day terms.

6. **Know your vendor's competitors – Take bids constantly:** After six months of working with a vendor and paying them promptly, make sure to understand the market, the names of their competitors, and get competitive quotes. You do not have to change vendors if the service is phenomenal, but you must act if the pricing difference is a material amount. In this case, bring your vendor into the office, mention you must keep the bidding competitive, but you need them to look at their pricing relative to ABC Company's lower bid on the same work. Never show a competitor's bid; this is very unethical but mention the vendor name to let your vendor know you know the market.

7. **You do not know everything – Ask your vendor how to save money:** Ask your vendor how he suggests you cut your costs? Maybe your specifications are too tight or restrictive, eliminating far cheaper alternative suppliers? Maybe your order quantities are too small causing setup costs to escalate your piece price? You may not know the best order quantity for the best price. Ask them to

review this and make sure to tell them they are getting the first chance at this cost reduction opportunity because you value their input.

19 Examples of Problems Your Receiving Personnel Need To Discover And Report

Teach all of your employees in the receiving department to understand that they are ensuring the company pays for items it ordered and no less. These are the issues that occur every day you want to teach these employees to spot and report BEFORE anxious delivery drivers leave. When your receiving people are short on help, teach them to call other departments to demand backup help to ensure they and their assigned help are able to do a thorough job at the time of delivery.

Here are some issues you want them to spot and bring to your attention before signing any delivery ticket or bill of lading.

1. Bad or faulty receipt of shipping supplies.

2. Incorrect or deficient load of quality control, laboratory or testing supplies or equipment.

3. Shortages or incomplete shipment of welding rods, metal and other various supplies.

4. Incorrect maintenance equipment and replacement parts.

5. Faulty cleaning agents or incorrect shipment of cleaning rags, wrong uniforms, industrial gases.

6. Shortage of screws, nuts, bolts, wood, plastic parts, metal fasteners.

7. Wrong sized replacement belts for company machinery.

8. Out of specification components, painting, finishing, packaging.

9. Incomplete or inadequate outside services.

10. Missed delivery deadlines of purchased parts or supplies.

11. Incorrect sized pallets or wrong size boxes and wrapping packages that do cannot contain our product or do not fit into the storage racks in the warehouse.

12. Wrong raw materials delivered in wrong sizes or types or grades.

13. Wrong chemicals and wrong quantities.

14. Expired products billed as new or fresh and current.

15. Leaking or punctured bags of chemicals, materials which were damaged originally by the vendors' drivers before they arrived at the plant.

16. Damage to employee automobiles by sloppy lawn care personnel or hit, damaged or backed into by onsite contractors' trucks or vehicles.

17. Parking lot damage incurred to cars or trucks or company buildings, sidewalk railings and fire hydrants stemming from customers' trucks driven carelessly.

18. Delivery men leaving prematurely and missing parts of the scheduled delivery still remaining on the truck.

19. Delivery men leaving without obtaining authorizing signatures of receipt and recording accurate dates

that product was actually dropped off and received at the company.

Involve and encourage all employees to spot problems. All employees need to be trained to report purchasing chargebacks or vendors' product failures. There are many things employees can be trained to do in order to save the company money. They need to be aware of their need to report when products and services are either not received as planned or they fail in service. Everyone knows when a purchase has gone awry. It needs to be reported that same day in order to notify the vendor.

Teach more than one person in your shipping department how to return purchases to company vendors. This requires, many times, getting approval from the company where the purchase started. Many require an authorization before you can ship anything back. Teach more than one person how to do this every day if necessary. All occurrences are reportable to purchasing for reimbursement and will save the company money.

Teach your employees about asking about warranties on company purchases. Teach your employees to inquire about maintenance warranties to see if your company is owed any money when a piece of equipment fails. When the vendor replaces a part, they should give the remaining on the other part that failed. This is most likely more familiar to people when their car batteries fail. Most know the battery carries a multi-year warranty towards the purchase of the next battery.

37 Sample Questions To Ask Receiving Dock Personnel

Select the appropriate questions for your company to ask for your receiving dock personnel and note where they need training.

1. Are you aware of the receipt of wrong sized replacement belts for company machinery?

2. Do you know if the company received out of specification components, painting, finishing or packaging?

3. Did the company order and receive incomplete or inadequate outside services (i.e. Painting, coating, finishing, lawn care, roof repair, AC service, duct cleaning, plumbing repair, etc.)?

4. Do you know the procedure to report missing work, job discrepancies, incomplete work or anything else that the company paid for but did not receive?

5. Are you aware of any vendor that missed our company's mandated shipment deadlines on purchased parts or supplies? Did you report the missed deadline?

6. Were you instructed not to say anything about problems on the receiving dock? Do you know who to inform these problems in Purchasing?

7. Are you aware of any receipt of incorrect sized pallets or wrong size boxes and wrapping packages that cannot contain our product or do not fit into the storage racks in the warehouse?

8. Are you aware of any receipt of wrong raw materials delivered in wrong sizes or types or grades?

9. Are you aware of the company receiving wrong chemicals and wrong quantities?

10. Did our firm order and receive expired products billed as new or fresh and current?

11. Did our company order and subsequently receive, leaking or punctured bags of chemicals, materials or other items damaged originally by the vendors' drivers before they arrived at the plant? Why did you happen to know they were leaking when they arrived at the plant yet not report it?

12. Did our company incur damage to employee automobiles by sloppy lawn care personnel (i.e. lawn mowers throwing rocks)?

13. Were any of our facilities hit, damaged or backed into by onsite contractors' trucks or vehicles? Did you get the vendor's name? If not, did you get a license plate number? Who handles this?

14. Did our company have any parking lot damage incurred by outside truck drivers? Did they do any damage to cars or trucks or company buildings, sidewalk railings and fire hydrants stemming from careless driving they did not report?

15. Are you aware of any delivery men leaving prematurely and missing parts of the scheduled delivery still remaining on the truck?

16. Are you aware of any delivery men leaving without obtaining authorizing signatures of receipt and recording accurate dates that product was actually dropped off and received at the company?

17. What companies drop off goods and ask for no signature?

18. Are you aware of a receipt of bad or faulty shipping supplies?

19. Are you aware of an incorrect or deficient load of quality control, laboratory or testing supplies or equipment?

20. Are you aware of a shortage or incomplete shipment of welding rods, metal and other various supplies?

21. Are you aware of a receipt of faulty cleaning agents or an incorrect shipment of cleaning rags, wrong uniforms or industrial gases?

22. Are you aware of a short shipment of screws, nuts, bolts, wood, plastic parts or metal fasteners?

23. Are you aware of the receipt of incorrect maintenance equipment and replacement parts? Do you know how to report them?

24. Do you document your outside vendor problems and demand restitution? Do you know the procedure? If you do not do this, who is assigned to this task?

25. Do you know how to report receiving shortages on the day received while the truck is still in the dock? If you do not, who does?

26. How often do you let the trucks leave and then count items later (even though you approved the shipping manifest and all of its counts)? Who authorized you to do this?

27. Do you know how to report receiving shortages several weeks after the load has been accepted?

28. When you are busy, are you forced to skip counting procedures when trucks are lined up and waiting?

29. Have you been instructed to skip some procedures at times when work backs up and there is no additional help made available? Does this happen frequently?

30. Do you ever find discrepancies months later when boxes are opened that were ignored the day they were originally received? If so, do you report this to purchasing? If you do not, are you told it is too late to report shortages? Do you know it is never too late to report shortages?

31. Were you taught that all shortages regardless of age need to be reported to purchasing so that they can file a claim with the supplier? There are no exceptions to this for you working in receiving.

32. As a receiving person in the receiving department, are there times when the work load becomes too heavy, everyone is busy in receiving and you need one or two extra people for the additional load? When that backlog occurs, what do you do?

33. As a receiving person, on days when it is very busy and trucks are backed up, if you ask, do you get the

extra help for the time needed to properly receive all incoming shipments? If not, are you told the reason?

34. When it is busy in your department on days with multiple truck loads and lots of different difficult parts to count, are there times that you are unsure if the company received everything that was ordered?

35. As a receiving person, do you physically count everything that comes through the receiving dock? If you do not count the items yourself, who helps on days when you are short of help?

36. Do you ask for help on busy receiving days?

37. Where do you believe there is the most risk in the receiving department?

Receiving Good Practices:

Teach receiving people how to independently verify what was supposedly received and not use the supplied bill of lading by the driver of the truck. Make sure you got what your company ordered.

Count products that are delivered to your company separately from shipping manifests that the driver brings with the load. You do not know if everything is there just because it is written down on a piece of paper created by someone anxious to go home.

Report immediately any shortages to Purchasing so they can have the bill of lading corrected and the vendor notified their paperwork is incorrect.

8 Questions To Ask About Company Advertisements

Ask these questions at no expense. Ask your employees what they think of your advertisements.

1. **What is your first gut reaction to our advertisement?** Ask this question often. If the employees truly do not think the current ads are effective, what do they suggest? What do they prefer? Get their feedback. Ask them to speak up. Give them plenty of opportunity to respond. If you have to, get a third party to ask them questions and allow them to answer them anonymously. Why? They will confuse their answers to your questions while thinking about their paychecks. You do not want this. You want blunt honesty.

2. **Rate our advertisement one to ten and be honest.** Consider keeping an open suggestion box reserved for reactions reserved for the company's advertisements so employees can make comments about changing ads. Ask for ongoing feedback while the companies commercials run on radio, television, cable or ads are placed in your newspaper. Put a picture of the current ad or text on the suggestion box to remind participating employees of the current commercial and ask what they think about it this week. Ask them to rank them. How do you rate this week's ad? (1 to 5, 5 being the best, 1 being a dog - woof) and add a suggestion to make the ad more relevant or to add punch.

3. **What is missing from this advertisement?** Where, what and when do you think we should advertise that we are not doing right now?

4. **Who is missing who might be targeted?** What groups do you think we are missing that might be interested in our product? Who do you think would like our product or service that we have forgotten?

5. **Did you like it; yes or no?** Did you like the advertising you saw for the company's product or not? If not, what was wrong with it?

6. **What type of advertising do you prefer?** The company's ads may be pointed to a very limited audience, so the general public may not be affected or care about your products or services.

7. **Is the use of the company product clearly demonstrated for the viewer?** Does the product that the company makes have a lot of uses? Does our advertising convey all of the uses for our products? Are all of those uses shown in pictures for advertising? If not, what uses or great attributes are those ads missing?

8. **Describe an advertisement you saw that you liked.** Which company was the sponsor and what were they selling (if you can remember)?

17 Advertising Ideas To Try Including Using Your Front Lobby

1. Are there free giveaways, little but interesting promotional freebies centered totally on company products and services sitting in plain sight in the company's front entrance where everyone enters the building?

2. Is there a reason why you would not want people to know what you do? If not, why not feature your products in the front entrance? Put your products in front of them. The problem with most of the public lies in their inability to imagine what you do by just listening to your words. Show them pictures and leave no doubt.

3. If you do not have any freebies or promotional items, get some marketing people on it. You want people to take things away with your name and telephone number on them. (i.e. calendars, key chains, guides, helpful hints or suggestions listings, etc.)

4. Are there handouts (brochures / catalogs / lists of services, pamphlets, business cards, sample products) that are offered to visitors?

5. What is the reason you do not want to have any printed material someone could take with them? What possible reason would you not want visitors to know what the company does? Suggestion: If you do not know what to write, get a copy of your company letterhead, enter the heading, "Examples of Our Products", and write down a list of the last

twenty or thirty items in full description sent to current customers. Assign someone to keep track of these shipments and to assemble this listing. Ask the shipping department to give you a list. Write it up neatly, copy it off 100 times and hand it out until your marketing department can wake up.

6. If you do have them available, are these product or service publications easy to find or do visitors have to look for them or ask for them? You understand that most will not ask for something they cannot see. Even if you do not want to keep them in the lobby, post a sign announcing you have brochures available upon request.

7. Are these flyers or pieces of literature offered under a sign that begs the visitor to take one "FREE – PLEASE TAKE ONE" This sign should be sitting in full view of visitors who come into your lobby. Any person coming into the front lobby should immediately see free literature or brochures offered in plain view for visitors. There is no reason why any rational marketing person would not do this free advertising at your own facility where interested parties are entering at any given time.

8. Are there plenty of enlarged photos of your products or services or photos of your products being used hanging on the walls or featured on the packaging of your product? Do those photos have good resolution? Are they shot at interesting angles? Is the company logo in full view?

9. Do the photos tell observers what the products do, how they are used, how they enhance the user's life, or make things easier or more enjoyable. Are there people shown using your various company products? Is the woman holding your product smiling or bored? If it is hard to tell, you failed.

10. Are the pamphlets or lists that are featured in racks or stands in your lobby plentiful, full of photos, sales contact names, business cards attached and easy to find?

11. Are those racks replenished every day with updated materials?

12. Is someone assigned to this duty and measured by it?

13. Is this same material available to your employees if they want to take it and give it out to family and friends?

14. Does your truck driver carry some company brochures in his cab and is he encouraged to pass them out? He sees a lot of people every day. Give him some. It may do no good or it might stir a lead. You have no idea how many people he speaks to every day in behalf of your company.

15. Do your sales people check in regularly to restock their supply of brochures to pass out?

16. Is this same promotional material made available to your vendors? They may not know what you can do. Are there some in your purchasing agent's

offices to pass out? Are vendors encouraged to take some with them if they wish?

17. Do you offer any referrals that stemmed from the distribution of literature in your lobby? You want every visitor that has taken the time to come to your facility to know more about what your firm can do. You want that visitor to tell someone else, pass on your brochures and spread your capabilities by word of mouth. You want free advertising. You want referrals. Your lobby must market for you and work for you, even when you are not there.

8 Places To Put Your Company Contact Information Which Are Easy For Customers To Find

Try considering these additional ideas for adding easy ways for your customers to contact you:

1. Print contact information on your shopping bags, boxes, shrink-wrap or pallet-boxes that go home with your consumers.

2. Print this contact information on your company business cards that your sales representatives hand out.

3. Print this information on the front door(s) of all of your facilities (especially for after-hour visitors who want to follow up with someone as soon as your door opens).

4. Feature your contact information on your company's vehicle door magnetic signs seen by thousands of cars across town. (i.e. autos, trucks, delivery vans, 18 wheelers, company truck beds, etc.).

5. Wherever possible, print your telephone number and website address on your products. Put this information directly on stickers adhered to the house air conditioners you serviced, hair shampoo bottles, dog food bags, nail polish samples, internal metal parts or components or anything that is not thrown away with the initial packaging. Include this information because you do not know why the customer might need it in the future. He may want

to find out how to reorder in a different location, or order in bulk, inquire about different product or service options or he may be asking in order to become a distributor.

6. Print your contact information on all company literature and brochures that are handed out.

7. Print your contact information on all company letterhead paper, envelopes, purchase order forms, company billing invoices, freight packing lists, shipping authorizations, sales acknowledgments, and any other document your company issues to customers.

8. Include your contact information on all your receipts that the customer takes home. (i.e. telephone number to ask about warranty information, return information, faulty product claims, etc.)

12 Examples Of Doing More Than You Promise For The Customer

Here are good examples of exceeding the company promise. Do these types of things regularly and your customers who are happy with the results will end up being your best advertising.

1. Promise a service call between 9 and 12 and **show up a few minutes before nine**; call the customer first and then ask if it is ok with them for your workers to start early.

2. Deliver items to your customers' homes earlier than **when they expect it**.

3. **Handle paperwork, forms, registrations and licenses for the customer**. Make what you deliver truly premium service. Take the headache away from buying or purchasing what you sell. Make everything easy about dealing with your firm.

4. If you deliver a new refrigerator, **offer to take the old one away** if your customer needs that service. Consider doing this for anything that is being sold that is replacing something already owned by the customer. They may want the old one but you do not know how many people do not buy the new one because they do not know what to do with the old one they have. Eliminate their worries and simultaneously make a sale.

5. If a car is being repaired, **take the person home** and have the car delivered if it is in the shop for major repairs. In fact, offer ultra-premium car

service that is performed at night with the car delivered to your driveway before you go to work the next morning; work done while you sleep.

6. When a manufactured item is shipped, **an email is sent to the buyer** that the truck just left the plant on its way to his designated shipping location. Have this programmed in your system so that it goes to multiple email addresses if the buyer chooses this option to be notified. Follow up with an email that states that the delivery was made and give them a 800 number if there are any problems with the delivery.

7. If you are hired to remove a tree from a yard, take all of the remaining debris in your truck. Rake the yard before leaving. Clean the yard and **leave it in better shape than when you found it**. Ask the owner to inspect your work before leaving and signing the work order.

8. If you clean carpets, **do the difficult work**. Move the furniture out and back into the rooms as part of the price, automatically. Leave a room freshener if possible and maybe let the customer determine a specific scent from a selection you offer beforehand upon taking the order.

9. If you sell baked pies, **offer a premium service** which includes a couple of paper plates, plastic utensils and a couple of napkins. Ultra-premium service includes a quart of vanilla ice cream and a scoop.

10. If you prepare tax returns, prepare and send a newsletter to your clients two or three months before yearend to provide a detailed list of "10 Best Ideas for Tax Planning BEFORE The Year Ends and You See Me!". Your **advice ahead of time will make you more money** than anything else you do since you will stand out and amaze your clients. Send this advice ahead of time. If you really want to get their attention, handwrite a couple of pieces of advice on their copy when you send it to personalize their listing concerning their own individual tax situations. You will relate to them personally and virtually guarantee their return business for your gesture.

11. If your company protests property taxes on behalf of your clients or companies, send a listing of tasks that can be done before yearend to cut the company's property taxes. It is useless to tell your clients after yearend since it is too late then to affect December 31st balances. Your suggestions will be talked about, passed around and most likely, you will pick up new customers who want a proactive firm working in their behalf also.

12. House cleaning staff can give their clients information gathered during their service. **Add value to your service**. They can prepare notes before they leave checking off the tasks that were done and noting those items that will be done the next time, or those items that could not be done.

Handwrite all of the issues noted that the homeowner needs to be aware of:

- Bathtub faucet dripping.
- Sounds noted from the attic (possible squirrels or pest infestation noted).
- Cracks noted in cleaned windows and casements.
- Air blowing in around door framings (losing heat, costing money).
- Evidence of water dripping along the wall behind appliances like the freezer or refrigerator.
- Areas of the carpet that are noted to be wet or smell from mildew.
- Areas of the flooring that seem to sag or creak (flooring needs inspection possibly).
- Odd cars sitting in the street that are normally not there (write down the license plate numbers in case this hunch pans out).
- Mention all service personnel that come to the house while the cleaning service is being performed (note their company names and vehicle license plate numbers for the owner).
- If something critical occurs, call the homeowner while you are at the house and inform them of the problem at their house.
- Lights or room ceiling fans that do not work, or especially note those electrical fixtures that are noted to flicker off and on as if from electrical 'shorts'.

7 Items To Include On Your Company's One Page Summary And 12 Suggestions For Distributing It

Sometimes customers appreciate a one-page summary versus a lot of pamphlets and literature they will not read. Get to the point with the handouts. Here are some items you should consider including in your company one page advertising summary.

1. Company logo, addresses and locations. If there are too many locations, write the cities. If there are too many cities, write "129 locations nationwide" or "34 manufacturing sites covering eight countries".

2. Company 800 number.

3. Company website.

4. Industries served.

5. Number of customers (i.e. 2,000 customers over the four-state area, 150+ utility companies across Texas panhandle, 34,000 customers in Scott County, 2,350 trucking firms have used our services for 43 years).

6. What does the company sell, make, process or distribute? For example, if your firm is a metal manufacturing, describe the types of processes performed and number and types of machines operated. If you own a toy company, how many and what types of toys do you make or sell, covering which age groups. If an insurance brokerage, what types of insurance coverage, dollar limitations, how much coverage currently in place (i.e. over $11.5B in place in 2015), how many

insurance companies used, what certifications or grades (i.e. A- and above, B or above) and how many locations owned.

7. Discuss the best and most impressive projects you have performed. For example for lawn care, "For over 10 years, we've cared for properties from only 600 square feet, all the way up to 1,750 acres with over 5,000 trees at the state fairgrounds." Another example might discuss completed welding projects as large as 110 feet long with 2,700 weld joints containing fourteen different metals.

What you should do with a one page company handout:

1. **Receptionist:** Give a copy to the receptionist so he or she knows the overall description of the company when answering general questions. She is also to offer these to every visitor, vendor, sales person, buyer or member of the public that walks into your lobby.

2. **Visitors:** Give out these flyers in the lobbies of all your facilities to all visitors.

3. **Delivery men:** Ask your drivers who know and see your customers every day to pass these summaries out to the buyers they contact regularly.

4. **Sales personnel:** Give out these handouts to help sales personnel. While they are introducing themselves, they can leave a well thought out summary description of the company's capabilities when talking to a new potential customer (with an attached business card at the upper left top corner).

5. **Current customers:** Make sure to give them to all your current customers. Sometimes they are the last to know your new capabilities since the sales representatives are telling primarily new prospects all of your new talents and abilities. Attach them with outgoing invoices. They will go through the mail free.

6. **Transportation personnel:** Offer these flyers to visiting truckers and drivers in shipping when they ask, "What all do you guys do here?"

7. **Vendors:** Purchasing agents should hand out these flyers to all the incoming vendors who want to bid on projects or do work for you. They end up hiring you if you offer something they also purchase.

8. **Accounts payable payments:** Put these one page handouts in vendors' accounts payable checks (stick in the envelopes) to mail every week.

9. **Invoices:** Slide these one page summaries in with all new invoices forwarded to your customers (stick in the envelopes).

10. **Attach to all emails:** Scan this company summary to electronically attach to all outgoing corporate emails. Leave it to the customer to open it if they so desire. If they wish to know what your firm does and you are bad at remembering all the details, this will do the trick.

11. **Facilities visitors (buyers, customer representatives):** Use this summary to give to any new visitor who arrives at your plant in order not to miss discussing everything you can do.

12. **Good cheap well written summary page:** One page is nothing to add to mail, and cheap to reproduce. Make plenty of copies, add a revision date at the bottom and continuously update your summary for new processes, products, capabilities, major projects, new services or products and numbers of locations, warehouses, store fronts and facilities.

Remember that you can get a lot on one page. Alter the font, organize the data neatly and understandably. Get to the point and make your concisely written copy have impact. Allow the one page restriction to help make you stick to the point and emphasize what truly is important to convey with one page.

10 Suggestions For Creating Your Picture Book Of Products And Their Benefits For The Consumer

Assemble a book full of photographs of your products being used in order to show customers your capabilities.

Here are some ideas to try when assembling your company picture book of products.

1. Assemble all of the pictures you have been taking of your products and services and have them bound or published (online) as a magazine or book. Minimize text and maximize the unique aspects of your products to share with customers.

2. Pass out copies of your photo magazine for your sales personnel to disburse to potential customers. Showing pictures will eliminate the possibility of the customer not understanding your capabilities.

3. Minimize the text. Describe in very few words what each photo represents; get to the point because most do not want or have time to read advertising. Show them.

4. Put the current year on the front of the magazine with the company name (i.e. 2020 ABC Company).

5. Try to obtain pictures of your products or services being used by your customers. Run a contest for customers and select the top 20 or 30 to include if warranted. Make sure to show new uses or your products used in new ways or methods. Your mission is to educate the potential buyers through pictures.

6. Show the readers your large and most difficult projects as well as the smallest and most simple.

7. Show readers complicated projects involving tremendous planning and execution to stress your company's deep capabilities.

8. Show them your products in action, stress, multiple uses and point out and visually demonstrate the benefits derived by the buyer directly in the photos.

9. Run a contest and pay your customers and employees for the best photos of product use. Put the best shots into a magazine to hand out to customers or to place in the lobbies of all of your facilities.

10. Put minimal text for explanations. Fewer words add punch and impact. Do not worry about writing a lot of copy to attempt to describe every boring detail you offer. Show potential buyers the results or benefits of buying from you. Demonstrate what your firm can do or offer or improve for all customers.

8 Cost Saving Ideas To Offer And Share With Your Customers

Any time you can help your customer and costs you nothing, give them the savings.

1. **Tips to save on property taxes.** Many times, purchasing personnel are linked to their inventory personnel so this cost savings opportunity will be welcomed if offered.

2. **Unique federal tax deductions for the current year.** The buyers may be interested in this to pass on to their accounting or tax department or they may not. This depends upon the size of their company. Small business owners who act as their company's buyer will appreciate this.

3. **Unique capital depreciation write-off opportunities about to expire.** If the buyer is involved with buying fixed assets (i.e. Computers, equipment, vehicles, etc.), he may be unaware of tax laws that change as of the 1st of January so he may appreciate the information shared with him.

4. **Common purchases opportunities.** If you know your buyer purchases the same raw material that you do and you are aware of a company that is deeply discounting their stock to get it moved before yearend, you may want to let the buyer know of this opportunity. If he is on any incentive program to drive down unit costs, he will appreciate the notification and company name and telephone number. This is a great double hit; a plus for your vendor and a plus for your client.

5. **Common administrative costs.** If you become aware of savings for low cost office supplies, reduced freight costs, lower sales tax savings, reduced outside service expenses or any other type of plant or company service or supplies savings, share it with your customer's buyer to help him.

6. **Freight company discounts.** Some freight companies offer discounts to their customers who forward them to new customers. If you are smart, tell the freight company you are forgoing the discount and you want your buyer to get it. Inform the buyer of this opportunity and make some point with him.

7. **Offer your vendors to your buyers for competitive bids.** Tell the buyer when he wants competitive bids for non-associated products and services to call you and you will forward your vendors to him. Tell him you will instruct your vendors they must give him an excellent deal because he is your customer. Your vendors will get the message and appreciate the potential business. Make your referral work for you.

8. **Banking opportunities sometimes arise.** Your loan representative for your company may approach you with cheap money and offer to pay off all of your higher interest rate loans at a low rate. This offer may also be eligible to outside firms as well so this would be an opportunity to pass this on to a customer if it seemed attractive.

Allow your customer to decide if they wish to make any of these cost savings contacts you offer on a regular

basis. In the case where a buyer may not express interest, never give your vendors' names out first. First tell your customers you want to help them potentially get more business or save money. Allow them to agree first. Once you have their permission, only then forward their contact information to your client.

Do not 'push' your customer; let him decide. You do not want a vendor bothering your customer when it is unwelcome. Tell the customer, "Here is the contact information if you decide you would be interested. Never worry, I do not give your name out unless you tell me first. It is your decision if you wish to make the contact." The buyer will appreciate your professionalism.

17 Cost Reductions, Suggestions Or Actions You Can Share With Customers

When you are able to pass on cost savings with your customer, do so. You will want to help those vendors of yours who helped you save money. They best thing you can do is **give them referrals.**

Here are some examples to follow.

1. Excellent tax return preparation agencies.

2. Reliable local transportation companies.

3. Long haul freight companies.

4. Local delivery services.

5. Local courier services.

6. Uniforms, rugs and production rags.

7. Food delivery services.

8. Low cost office supplies.

9. Great sources for used pallets.

10. Vendors for lawn maintenance or building maintenance.

11. Painters.

12. All forms of outside services. (i.e. Heat-treating, sawing metal, finishing, plating services, assembly work, payroll services, customs agents, etc.)

13. Banks for lines of credit.

14. Capital leasing companies with desirable interest rates.

15. Banks that will pay off debts and replace with cheaper interest rate monies and desirable payoff periods.

16. Printing companies (i.e. Brochures, inventory tags, shipping labels and manual instructions).

17. Competitive scrap companies (i.e. Wood, metal, plastics).

15 Questions To Ask About Your Company Recorded Message When Customers Are On Hold

When a customer calls your company and is put on hold, what does he hear? If you do not know, listen to what follows after being put on hold and ask yourself and others these questions, then do not hesitate to make the necessary changes to the company's recorded message.

Ask these questions often:

1. Is your message current?

2. Are there any contact information errors? (i.e. wrong telephone numbers, bad email addresses, websites that are closed, etc.)

3. Is your message relevant?

4. Does it talk about the company as it is today, or 10 years ago?

5. Does the recording discuss anything current that the firm should be touting?

6. Does it mention anything the customer may have heard in the news? If not, why not?

7. Does the recording mention the firm's website correctly?

8. Is there any mention of current new products, services or new features of your company?

9. Is the recording too loud or more bothersome than informative and helpful?

10. Have you had any independent parties give you feedback?

11. Have the receptionist keep a log of any comments made by customers (positive and negative) about the recording for review.

12. Does the recording give correct information (i.e. Website, telephone number for day and after hours)?

13. How long has it been since your company recording has been changed?

14. Would light music be more appropriate versus dialogue?

15. When the receptionist returns to the caller and transfers him to his party, does she mention the direct number so the caller can call direct the next time?

13 Reasons To Bill Customers Less Than You Quoted

The best thing to be is honest with potential customers. Quoting them a price should not cause distrust between you and him when he gets your final invoice. Make sure to give him the best and most accurate quote first and then, when the work is finished, present him an invoice equal to or less than that quote. You will create a new customer when that occurs. Follow these steps.

1. He does not expect fair treatment, given other bad incidents he may have endured from other unscrupulous vendors prior to your arrival.

2. He is thinking of your higher dollar figure on the quote until he sees your lower invoice amount.

3. Your lower final invoice amount did not abuse him; he's stunned and also instantly happy. This is how you want a customer to leave your firm, in a good mood.

4. He will leave smiling and relaxed.

5. He will have a better attitude at the final time of payment.

6. He will feel he was treated fairly.

7. When you bill him less than he expects, this event feels, to him, the same as if you handed him money.

8. He will most likely return now that you did not disappoint him.

9. He will think of you positively in the future.

10. You helped him and he will not forget it.

11. He will give you great referrals, if not more work himself.

12. He will advertise you freely and willingly, with no provocation from you because you gave him good work, a very fair price and did not take advantage of him when he was the most vulnerable as a customer.

13. You proved yourself as a trustworthy and honest vendor and he most likely will stick with you because you were honest with him.

29 Questions To Ask Distributors About Problems Or Suggestions About Your Products

Questions to ask your distributor drivers concerning their opinions about the market and how our company fares against the competition:

1. When you place our products in store displays, do you feel our company's packaging is better than normal, adequate or substandard?

2. Do our products show or display well or poorly in stores where you place products?

3. Do our products sell well in the stores where you place product?

4. Do our products look bad, good, average, boring compared to the competition?

5. Does the company's product packaging tear up easily while being moved or handled while making deliveries? Should it be upgraded, strengthened, shrink-wrapped more, packaged differently, different material, stronger wrapper, binding, etc.?

6. Do our products look cheaper or more expensive than those alternatives displayed nearby? Is that important in this market?

7. Is there anything about our products that seem unattractive or needs updating or improving? Tell us your suggestions in detail. (i.e. lime green mouthwash does not seem refreshing, Black Jell-O may not be appealing or appetizing, purple gravy

does not look good, directions on the medicine bottle printed with font too small for the elderly, directions in English only, toys too small for under three, pasta packaging with worms as mascots or advertising product icons?)

8. Do our products seem to be well marketed in general? Are they placed in the right stores? Should we consider something or somewhere different?

9. Compared to competitor products, what do our products need to be more competitive, more attractive or more appealing to the consumer? What are we missing?

10. Do you have more, same or less products with our company's products? Describe the differences about our product?

11. Is the product color attractive compared to the competitors? More? Less?

12. Is the product appearance fresh, outdated, average, boring, non-inviting, interesting, understandable, etc.?

13. Is there a feature that our company product has that no one else has, that is an attribute not currently advertised? Do you notice anything that makes our product a better value than the competitors that we do not mention in the advertising on the packaging (missed)?

14. Do you have any particular problems with our products that you do not have with others? (i.e. packaging, shelf life, bad instructions, etc.)

15. Is it difficult handling, moving, gathering, assembling, pushing or pulling our product for any reason? (i.e. samples of problems: vacuum sweepers hard to push on carpet, drivers' seats that are uncomfortable, lawnmower steering wheel that leaves marks on your hands when you perspire outside, electronic dashboards that are hard to figure out for the car owner, alarm clock that is difficult to set, cookware handles that rust or discolor when washed with bleach, cookware handles that are too hot and burn your fingers, dog bowls that tip over too easily)

16. Is there something that we could do that would make distribution easier? Different packaging? Different item count in standard size shipping containers or boxes?

17. You probably see a lot of products as a distributor. You see good products and bad products. Given your background are there any good attributes of our competitors' products that you like that we should consider? How do we size up to the competition?

18. What does our company need to do to improve and increase market share?

19. Are the profit margins on the market we are in tightening? Are they getting worse?

20. Do you see more and more competitors in our company's market, the same number or less? What new products out there are cutting into our market?

21. Who are the new competitors in the market that you see are potentially cutting into our market share? If you do not know exactly, guess or give us your best estimate of who has jumped into the marketplace.

22. If our company was to consider something beneficial or helpful to add to the current product that would make it a better value or more attractive, what would you suggest? (i.e. plastic spoon for yogurt, sprinkles in a cup for ice cream, dog bone treat sample attached to a bag of dog food, ten free CDs given with the purchase of a new stereo, a ream of paper with a new computer printer, a plastic filling cup for your gas tank with the purchase of a gas can or oil change, tie with a shirt, shirt and tie with a new suit, nail file with nail polish, nail glitter with nail polish)

23. What are the trends in the industry that our company is behind that we might consider?

24. What trend do you see that we will want to be certain NOT to join or participate that may long-term be detrimental in the market?

25. Do the customers that you service complain, comment or praise our products?

26. What do your customers ask you for regularly and consistently?

27. Is there anything that you can suggest to my company that we should consider changing, upgrading or eliminating about our products in order to grow our market share?

28. As a distributor, do you hear any customer comments about our products? If so, what are they? Describe their comments good or bad about our products.

29. What percentage of our product do you track?

7 Alternative Options To Consider And Offer When Your Customer Balks At Proposed Price Increases

Some customers balk at price increases regardless how long it has been since you last raised pricing. Instead of raising prices directly, here are some indirect methods to accept other cost cuts in exchange for not raising prices in order to increase your company's gross profit margins. Try one or more of these ideas.

1. **Volume Increases/ Process Reviews/ Redesign Options:** Tell him to order two or three times the volume and you may be able to give him a volume discount given that setup costs are the same regardless of the volume run. Are there parts or services you provide to him that can be made cheaper if he orders in a different manner or different time (i.e. Middle of the month versus month end, order services all together with lower overall costs incurred). Look at all of the tasks your firm does to complete a product, offer a service and think about stripping it down to bare bones to cut out costs. What processes can be eliminated that do not really affect the viability of the product? What can be changed in the manufacturing process that speeds up production, cuts labor costs, reduces scrap, eliminates finishing, painting, rubbing, edging, trimming, outside services, inspection time or any other task that if reduced in time or labor hours involved will cut your cost IF accepted by the customer?

2. **Packaging:** Suggest different, cheaper, packaging ideas, lower cost shipping methods or no packaging or freight at all (i.e. Let the customer come pick up the parts, strap the parts or products to a returnable pallet, package in a reusable wrapper, box, etc.). Can the packaging provided to the customer be cheapened? (i.e. Lower cost materials, no printing, wrapper comes on a roll).

3. **Freight:** Tell the customer you will drop the price if he picks up the product, saving on your freight costs with your driver or an outside carrier. Instead overnight delivery, allow a four or five-day shipping window (lessening the freight bill). If delivery date does not matter, go rail versus truck for long hauls. Give the customer a better rate if you are simply restocking a warehouse and have extra time versus fulfilling their current orders.

4. **Order Size/ Combination:** Ask him to order other products and increase the order size and you might be able to provide some discounts. Ask the customer to increase the order size so this reduces the setup time required for any order (fixed cost spread over a larger denominator of products produced). Ask your engineers, for a particular customer, what would be the most cost efficient order combination that could be obtained to drive down manufacturing costs; and then take this model to offer a reduced price for these combinations of order mix of products.

5. **Stock inventory/Guarantee buybacks:** Ask your customer to allow you to make stock to be put on

your shelves and held, but he must pay carrying costs while you are holding it for him (after an established period of time), and guarantee to buy it all in the event he leaves for another vendor.

6. **Early payment discounts for AR and AP:** Offer an early payment discount to your customer (i.e. Pays in 10 days versus 60) and at the same time, take advantage of early payment discounts worked out with your own vendors associated with this account.

7. **Buy from your customers:** Your customer might sell something you can use, and if cajoled, may be willing to sell it to you at cost in exchange for a price freeze on your product purchases for an equal amount of time. See if you can reach an agreement with him to get a deal you both like and instead of gaining more, you enjoy a healthy cost reduction on the purchasing side of the income statement. More money is more money, right?

Work with the customer and tell him you want a resolution to the proposed price increase that he can accept but no matter what, be clear; your firm cannot absorb all price increases forever.

11 Questions To Ask Customers To Find Out Why They Bought Our Product

You may think you know but you need to ask the customer why he bought your product. You need to clarify what caused his buying decision because if it is predominant in the customer responses you receive, you need to market to that group of buyers.

Here are some sample questions you might consider asking your buyers.

1. Is this your first time buying our product?

2. Did you buy our product because of price?

3. Did you buy our product because of our company's customer service?

4. Did our employees make buying from us easy or difficult?

5. What happened during your buying experience that you want to be improved on your next purchase?

6. Was there any aspect of the purchase that angered or perturbed you in any way? Tell us and we will review it for you.

7. Did you buy our product because of where the item was sold?

8. Was your decision based upon the convincing packaging?

9. Did a salesperson explain the product or service well or was the explanation deceiving?

10. Were you satisfied by the product or service? Why or why not?

11. Most important question to ask after purchase: ***Would you buy the product again? If not, why not?***

Ask your current buyers and customers these questions. They may announce reasons that you never considered and should start today in your marketing program.

Get these answers as quickly as possible and make the necessary changes to your marketing as needed.

12 Questions To Ask Ex-Customers About Why They Left

You need to know why customers buy from you but more importantly, you need to know why they left you and did not return. This is important and should be pursued every day so you may improve.

Read these questions and select those that seem to fit your company's needs.

1. What was the main reason you did not buy this product or service again or a second time?

2. What was missing from the product that caused disappointment and provoked the decision not to make a purchase a second time?

3. What change or item added or subtracted to the current product might make you think again, and buy it the second time? (i.e. did not taste good, product did not work very well, product too heavy to handle, product is not the right color, service provided was inadequate or not well performed, product breaks easily around kids, product is slightly overpriced, hard to find in stores).

4. What about the current product lets you down or is disappointing to you?

5. Does our product eliminate a problem or an annoyance in life for you, the buyer?

6. How does this product make things easier for you, more fun, or a little more enjoyable or reduce or eliminate a previously tedious and boring task?

7. What are the benefits of this product in your opinion? Versus the features?

8. Do the display cases that are used to show our product look cheaper than the product or the opposite?

9. How do the display cases look to you? How did you initially react?

10. Does the packaging enhance the perceived value of the product or diminish it?

11. When you see the packaging, does it clearly picture or demonstrate through illustrations how to use the product?

12. Is the packaging clear and does it convey the necessary message for even those who do not speak English?

19 Questions To Ask Employees Or Potential Customers About The Good And Bad Attributes Of Your Products

When you can, ask these questions to get market feedback and ideas for improvements to your products in the future. Select those that fit your company's needs.

1. Do you like this color for this product? If not, what would you change?

2. Do you like the current packaging for this product? If not, what would you change?

3. Do you think this product looks attractive to the average buyer? If not, what one or two things do you think would be easy to change right away about the product that would make a key difference to buyers?

4. If you do not like the current color of the product, what color would you prefer and consider buying if changed? What color do you personally prefer for this product?

5. Excuse me for a moment; let me grab a pen and paper and write down the specifics of the problem you had with our customer service today. I can say that they are short of staff right now and we do want them to improve so we take comments like yours seriously. I also want to get your name and call back number so a person can contact you today to resolve this issue with your purchase. Okay, I am ready to write. (*Show interest and give the customer the benefit of the doubt; do not act as a*

third party. Remember that this is the guy that pays your paycheck every two weeks.)

6. Do you like the finish of the product or is it unattractive? If you do not like the current finish of the product, what type of finish do you think would look better? Do you have a preference?

7. Would this product look good or fit well in your house or apartment? If you do not think so, tell us why specifically. (*i.e. too expensive, wrong color, wrong type or does not fit theme or type of furniture, too large, too small, too dangerous for kids, too dull, takes up too much space, etc.*)

8. If you had this product in your home, would this be popular among your family or circle of friends? Do their opinions matter to you for this type of purchase? *NOTE: Ask specifics because everyone generally has an opinion.*

9. What is the first thing that comes to mind when I ask you if you could make a change to our product?

10. Without thinking or dwelling too long on this question, quickly tell me your very first thought about improving the company product? Do you see a need? If yes, would you change it? What would you change to make it more appealing or useful?

11. Have you spoken to your friends or family about this product or one similar? If so, what was discussed? What problems were discussed that could help us to improve the product that we offer versus others in the market?

12. What about the product is too sharp or too rough or does not seem to be finished?

13. Is there something about the product that seems to be missing something or could be slightly changed to make it more comfortable to hold, handle or operate?

14. Do our products seem safe to you personally? Do they seem safe enough to buy them yourself?

15. Do the products you tried and tested seem to be safe for children to use? If not, what about the product is not child-proof or child-safe? What could be changed to eliminate this as a problem for potential buyers?

16. What can we do to show the buyer that this product is good for them? What types of pictures do you suggest we feature to convey the benefits of buying this product?

17. What do you think are a couple of major attributes that are appealing and make the buyer want to buy this product? Even if you do not buy the product, what do you think would be appealing to buyers in general?

18. What do you think are the major attributes that are NOT appealing and makes the buyer NOT buy this product? What is the major detriment of this product?

19. Do you think changing packaging to reflect the holidays is good for selling our product? Do you think it detracts from the product or adds to it?

15 Questions To Ask Your Customers Before They Hang Up

When your inside sales personnel are on the telephone with customers talking directly about your company products, ask one last question before the customer hangs up to see if they might have a good idea to use about your products.

Read these samples and choose one to ask every day before the customers hang up.

1. What different color do you think the product might be? What color are we missing?

2. What makes this product unique from others you mentioned you have previously purchased? What causes a problem with this product as you see it? Would you mind expanding on that?

3. What needs to be sold with this product? Something that would be helpful or complement the product?

4. What can be added or subtracted that makes the product more valuable?

5. What different surface treatment would be better or interesting?

6. What different size should we try?

7. What different finish should we try or offer?

8. What different use should we advertise that is applicable for this product or that which no one has thought of?

9. Should we photograph this product being used in a different place than normal?

10. How would you show this product being advertised?

11. What is the best thing about this product?

12. What is the worst thing about this product?

13. What needs to be added or modified?

14. What needs to be cut off or eliminated or redesigned do you think?

15. What needs to be filed down, smoothed out, unwrinkled, cleared, treated, bleached out, trimmed, straightened or bent?

Pick one or two questions and ask it over a period of time and observe trends in the answers and reactions.

21 Examples Of Questions When Customers Are Requested To Finish The Sentence "I Wish ..."

Ask your customers to finish or complete a "I Wish....." card to get ideas for improving customer service:

1. I wish you had **longer hours during the week**; I cannot get here through the traffic before you close. (Review store revenue by time periods and consider changing or extending store hours, especially if this comment occurs frequently or your competitors close earlier than you.)

2. I wish your **website wasn't so confusing**. I tried to buy something once but stopped; it did not seem very safe using my credit card. The main problem is that it is hard to understand what to do next. Your instructions are too vague, the buttons to click are too small, (why white buttons on a white background?) and when I do click something, nothing happens so I leave the website. It hangs up too often and the email box you provide does not work. I hope you are not paying a lot to someone to manage that site; if you are, you are being cheated.

3. I wish it was **easier to return defective products** in your store. I do not know why it takes so long; you are understaffed and the ones that do work there have no authority; they must call a manager from the back of the store every time. Who set up this process? It is not working.

4. I wish your **sale items were more clearly marked**. More than once when I take items to the counter, they charge me the wrong price. (Who is responsible for marking products? Check and review the job description and discuss the task with the employee. Bad prices ruin customer loyalty and embarrass buyers who have to call out your employees' errors.)

5. I wish you would **mark 'sale items' with the right prices**. I have to argue with the clerk at checkout to get the right price because they are not marked, so when this happens, everyone is held up in line. I hate to buy anything when you have to deal with this unnecessary hassle.

6. I wish you had the new fall pullover sweaters in the front of the store **offered in at least a couple of shades of red**. Did you talk to anyone about the new colors that are out this year? (Who is your buyer and can he buy more colors quickly in the event this comment is valid and was received several times?)

7. I wish you had an **easier bag to carry**; this stiff paper handles cut into the carrier's hands. Your competitor has a really easy to carry bag with plastic on the handle; they just started using them about a month ago. (Ask marketing people to review packaging and the distributor for packaging options in the market.)

8. I wish your **store was not so cold** with the air conditioning; the air blows directly down on you

when standing in line to check out. I know it is a little thing, but three people plus the clerk checking me out said the same thing. (See if an air deflector can be installed to divert air flow.)

9. I wish you had a **security guard in the parking lot** since there are no outside lights. I do not feel really safe outside after dark. (Who can be assigned after dark to make trips out to the lot or to escort shoppers from the front of the store?)

10. I wish it was **easier to get hold of someone** when I call the store. No one picks up even after I get a recorded message and try to hit "0". (What is the procedure and who is assigned in the front office to handle incoming calls? When that person is not working, who is the alternative?)

11. I wish you had an **extra person in the shoe department**. The man back there tries his best, but five or six people are waiting on one person and then you have personnel standing in other departments talking.

12. I wish someone would **respond when I send email inquiries** on your website. Sometimes I get a response but it is only a computerized general answer and does not answer my question. It is not worth trying to email anything when you cannot reach anyone.

13. I wish I could get some **help in your billings department** to get my account straightened out. One time my check cleared the bank and I showed this to your manager, but no one credited my

account. The next time I came to the store, the manager changed and I had to start the process over.

14. I wish I could **push a buzzer in the aisle or department to call for help** (an employee or clerk) to help me when I have a question about a product. I cannot find anyone, and then by the time I get to the front of the store, I just go ahead and leave because it is useless to try to get anyone's attention.

15. I wish it was as **easy to get out of your store** as it is getting into your store. I hate to come in and find anything I want to buy because it is a hassle to pay for it.

16. I wish someone would offer to help; I look at your employees and they ignore me.

17. I wish I could **look up products on a simple keyboard** at the front of your store when I enter; something really simple where I enter four or five characters and it looks up the matching words and tells me the aisles or locations in the store, maybe with a simple map from where I am standing. It takes forever to find anybody and they normally say they don't know the part of the store that I ask about.

18. I wish you guys would **smile occasionally**. Too many people look depressed. I sometimes wonder about my safety in your store given the type of employees you have hired. They act bothered when I ask a question.

19. I wish there was an **easy way to get product instructions after I get home.** My problem is that I

cannot find how to, 1. put my product together, 2. wash the piece of clothing I bought, 3. where to buy replacement parts, bulbs, fixtures, etc., 4. how to contact a repairman for this product, 5. how to contact the manufacturer. Is there an 800 number for these types of questions?

20. I wish your people were more **friendly when they answer the telephone**. They talk so fast, I cannot understand what they are saying. If they are busy, they cut me off or put me on hold. Am I the only one who has problems with getting through to someone in your organization? One day when the young lady cut me off, I simply called your competitor to place the $50,000 order. I did not know if you wanted to know that or not. I don't even like to deal with your competition, but in a way, you forced me to call them, didn't you?

21. I wish I could ask someone there for a **history of what I have purchased over the last 12 months**. I bought some things but do not know their names. I wanted to buy some more but do not know the names of the articles. I wish I could see my purchases in chronological order. I asked someone this question once but they were certain this was impossible and if you did this for one, you would have to do it for everyone. I do not think that person is with you anymore.

14 Customer Answers To Your Request To Them To Finish The Sentence "I Don't Like..."

Give your customers an opportunity to complain about one particular thing after buying from your company. The answers will give you opportunities to improve. These are samples of what you may get.

1. I don't like having to wait to check out in some of your stores. It takes under a minute to get into your store and half an hour to get out. I hate coming to your store for this reason and avoid buying very much when I can.

2. I don't like having to try to figure out how much something costs on your receipts. They are hard to read. Someone did a lousy job designing this for your customers. Can't a customer just get a legible receipt?

3. I don't like having to search for someone who works in the store. I can never find anyone and when I do ask, they tell me that where I am standing is normally not their area, and then most of them hurry to walk off.

4. I don't like the mess you have to look through. No one seems to be assigned to straightening articles on the shelves. I would think someone is supposed to do this every day, right?

5. I don't like to have to wait to talk to someone. When waiting on the telephone, your background music is too loud and screechy and only makes me

mad having to wait for someone to pick up the telephone. If you cannot offer soothing or pleasant music as a backdrop, do not play any at all.

6. I don't like to park in your parking lot. It is too dark at night and I think I am going to be robbed.

7. I don't like to return purchased articles to your store. It takes a very long wait in line and when I do, they are not well trained. I thought you offered a money-back guarantee.

8. I don't like the hours you offer on Friday night. I work all week and can't shop in your store if you are going to close at 7pm on one of the busiest nights of the week? Who thought this schedule up?

9. I don't like to call wanting to place an order only to have to wait on hold, then be talked to like I am bothering your employees. What happened to customer service in your place? Do you not train your employees?

10. I don't like your website. It is hard to find anything. You sell light fixtures and I entered "lamp" into the search box and got NO RESULTS? Really, no results?

11. I don't like your product packaging and stickers. It is hard to get some of them off your products. Can't you find something easy to peel off without leaving a mark?

12. I don't like your product manuals. Who decided 6-point font was legible? When you ordered the instruction manuals, did anyone bother to look at

them and see if they were acceptable? Why would you think anyone can read this small print? Do you not have a large print manual available? Do you forget that half of your customers are seniors? We don't have good eye-sight but we do have money.

13. I don't like the color selections of your product that are displayed. Are there more available? If there are more options for the public, why not display the entire palette? Why are more hidden in the back?

14. I don't like the delivery service you hire. They came to my house, put the package on the ground and took off. They did not call as I requested. I thought someone would at least let me know the item I ordered was in and might give me an option to come pick it up? It happened to rain the day they left the box and it was soaked, and it ruined some of the material inside, which also happened to be poorly packaged. I have brought the entire box back and want a credit on my account.

Of These 26 Competitive Advantages, Pick Yours Out

Your company sells its products but may not know why its customers buy from them. Once you find out from customers what is causing them to buy from you, you can advertise your competitive advantages and gain more sales. You must first realize where you exceed and where you do not.

Read these competitive advantages, mark the ones that apply and create advertising that takes advantage of where you exceed.

1. You deliver faster than anyone.

2. You have more warehouses logistically spread across the country.

3. You have better packaging that can be recycled and used or is easier to unwrap or poses a function when products are held on pallets or a warehouse or in boxes, etc.

4. Your warranty is longer and more comprehensive than your competitors.

5. Your product is the same as the rest of the field, but it has almost no returns (dependability).

6. Your product can be ordered with free shipping.

7. With the purchase of your product, you throw in some freebies that the competition does not have.

8. Your 800 number is open 24/7 and tells you how much longer the caller must wait in order to talk to a person.

9. Your product, even though it functionally acts the same, is available in twice as many colors, patterns, sizes and packaging types.

10. You perform your service for the customer and then, before you leave the customer's facility, you notify the buyer and ask if there are any questions before leaving. You leave a list of things to do in the event of any problems. You leave the buyer feeling no remorse and confident he made a good purchase decision when he called you versus the competition.

11. Your manual that you provided comes in multiple languages. Your website can be read in multiple languages.

12. Your product has a longer shelf life.

13. Your product is regarded more 'green' than the other products. (i.e. environmentally friendly, less impact, less waste, etc.)

14. Your product is easier to operate, run, turn on, adjust, carry, install or have repaired.

15. You offer to provide some training to every customer for using, repairing and servicing your product.

16. You replace bad or defective parts immediately, unlike your competitors. You send emails with prepaid shipping labels so the customer does not have to pay for the company's mistakes.

17. You have some of the best and most knowledgeable sales people in the industry and do not know it.

18. Customers like it that a human voice answers your company telephone.

19. You are open conveniently during hours when the competition has gone home.

20. Your five-point guarantee (example) is to the point, rings with customers, alleviates customers' fears and concerns and provides enough rationale to the average buyer to justify buying your brand versus the competitor's.

21. Your store smells good.

22. Your store sounds nice (good soothing music, friendly help, easy to get in and get out).

23. Your store is open more hours than the rest.

24. Your people are the most knowledgeable.

25. Your return policy is the best.

26. Your warranty is the best.

11 Questions Designed To Encourage Your Customers To Complain

Learn something; ask your customers one or more of these questions, whichever seems appropriate. Alternate every week or so if you wish to get different or more detailed answers and suggestions (which is what you want from customers). The most important thing you can do is satisfy your customers so they will return. If they are not satisfied, you need to know it and you need to get them to tell you why they are disappointed. If they will not tell you, you have lost them so start asking questions, politely.

1. If there anything else I can help you with today, please let me know. If your request is something I might not know I have plenty of people I can get the answer for you, so do not hesitate to ask.

2. We appreciate your business so please let me know if there is anything else that you need. Do not hesitate to let me know; we cannot improve unless we ask you.

3. Please let me know if you have any questions about those items that are on sale. All of them are not on display; we have more in stock so let me know if you are interested as quickly as possible.

4. We need good feedback to continue to make improvements so let me know what you think. We appreciate the feedback.

5. In your opinion, what about this (product or service) would you change or alter to make it better?

6. When you run into problems with this, please call me; and I will do my best to help you.

7. Please let me know if you cannot find something or need some help. I am glad to be of assistance for you.

8. What aspect about this if you had the opportunity would you change do you think?

9. What is the first thing that came to mind when you saw this new product? Do you like the color, functionality, size, shape, finish, clever design, etc.?

10. Is there anything about this new item that you would change for you, personally, if you had your wish?

11. Before you go, is there anything else you need help with? Did you find everything you wished to look at today?

Check up on your company. Encourage your customers to voice their concerns and ask every time you have a chance, "Is there anything else that we can do for you?" Ask for customers' feedback and openly invite criticism every day. Customers who get to voice their disapproval are saying, "Let me validly complain and once I do, I am willing to give your company another chance. If I do not speak up about the problem I have with you, it is because I have given up on you and I am going elsewhere."

We greatly respect those companies which lead by doing. They deliver great products or deliver great service. We like and want to buy from those companies which back what they promise and deliver more than discussed, time after time. We also like those companies that pay attention to us and value what we say to them.

13 Questions To Ask Your Customers To Find Out "How Are We Doing?"

Train all of your employees to ask questions of customers to encourage good feedback. Here are some that you can pick out and try. Be prepared to discover a number of things you did not know bothers your customers. Try asking the following question that comes with various different endings shown below.

Question: Given your recent purchase, service or interaction with our company, what can our company ...?

1. Improve on?

2. Do differently?

3. Do faster?

4. Do more politely?

5. Ship more quickly?

6. Ship more safely?

7. Package differently?

8. Package more safely and securely?

9. Feature or explain more clearly?

10. Advertise more understandably?

11. Detail steps more clearly?

12. Call back or returns calls more quickly?

13. Help more completely?

...or if you are really at a loss for words, ask the simple question "How Are We Doing?"

13 Questions To Ask Previously Large Customers Concerning Why They Left?

If you are lucky enough to question the buyer of a large customer who decided to leave your firm or buy considerably less, ask him or her some of these example questions to find out why their firm turned to another source.

1. When we analyzed our business with your firm, it has not grown and we wondered what we neglected to do to win some new business?

2. What happened? What did we do wrong that you are no longer buying anything from us or at least as much as you used to?

3. What do we need to do in order to win your business again?

4. Did we tell you of our company growth, increase in capacity, production facilities, number of warehouses, offices and new products and services?

5. Did we give or show you a list of all of our new capabilities or product lines?

6. Did we mention our new machinery and equipment?

7. Did we tell you of our new locations or new branches?

8. Did we introduce you to our new sales personnel? (Maybe the customer hated, despised or at best tolerated your assigned salesperson in the past.

Sales personnel can be changed or switched if that is what is needed.)

9. Did we tell you, show you or demonstrate for you our new products or services? Did we give you samples, catalogs, brochures, idea lists, testimonials, instructions, videos or any other type of marketing or promotional item that might get your attention to our request?

10. Did we tell you about our new insurance limits and coverage? (This may have been a problem in the past.)

11. Did we offer you a plant tour of our new facilities?

12. Can we rebid some of your products or services needed?

13. Even if you are no longer interested in doing any business with our firm, what was the primary reason why you chose another firm? It is good for us to know so we can change our approach and training of our staff.

9 Examples Of How To Educate Your Customers To Save Money So You Will Make More Of It

Share with customers how to save or make money and they will come back to you for more advice in the future because they will remember who told them. Here are some examples of methods of teaching customers something of value for various businesses.

1. Teach your customers how to store food items once opened in order to stretch their food dollar. Add this as an instructional sticker on the food package or post the preservation notice in the produce section.

2. Teach your customers how to change and add the correct amount of oil to their car. Consider holding classes to instruct customers how to perform this task on their car.

3. Teach your customer to add the correct amount of air to their tires and subsequently how to measure it. Give them a flat tire and tell them to go at it.

4. Teach your customer how to prepare a wall for sanding, base coat and paint before they leave the store. Let them practice on a demonstration wall if desired.

5. Teach your customers how to make their own salsa in the produce department while you sell them the ingredients. Let them have the first batch purchase at 30% off so they can see and taste their savings.

6. Teach people how to use power tools to do tasks at home themselves while you sell them the tools,

nails, screws and other hardware they will be
buying.

7. Teach people how to use a carpet shampooer and
sell them all of the hardware and liquid cleaner. Let
them shampoo a carpet in the store and show them
how to use the machine. Let them operate it just
before they are then convinced to buy one.

8. Teach people how to cultivate indoor and outdoor
plants before selling them plant food, pots, fertilizer
and seeds. Give them instructions with every plant
how to feed, water and gather seeds to produce
more plants. Give them future discount coupons for
free plants and seeds during the next growing
season.

9. Teach people how to repair their lawnmowers, add
oil, change blades, sharpen blades, remove broken
guards or belts. Do this before they buy planters,
weed-eaters, edgers, walk-behind mowers or any of
the hundreds of parts these machines require.

36 Questions To Ask Your Potential Customers

Train your sales personnel to encourage their potential customer contacts to speak up and voice their concerns about choosing your firm. Here are some questions to select to ask those important contacts.

1. What could get in the way of getting an agreement with our company done today?

2. What criteria would you use to choose a replacement firm versus using our company?

3. What details do you want explained that we did fully talk about?

4. What do you see as the greatest risks in making this purchase decision for your firm?

5. What do you see as the primary benefits of our company's product/solution? Do you see any other potential benefits?

6. What concerns do you have if you decide ultimately to buy from us?

7. What do you want to happen that is not now happening within my company?

8. What does it take to be successful in your position?

9. What else do we need to discuss to satisfy your concerns?

10. How did you first find out about us?

11. Are there companies that you see as our competitors? (If YES, ask for the top two or three that come to mind.)

12. How did you first become aware of these alternative companies? (This may be different for each.)

13. When you were shopping for <u>your product</u> and you selected us, what did you look for in vendor?

14. Did you consider any alternatives to (name of your company)? If so, how did you make your decision?

15. What was the number one thing or concern that caused you to choose our company when making your decision?

16. Thinking back to when you made your purchase decision, is there anything you saw about us that especially helped you decide to buy from us? (A brochure? News article? Our website? Another online source? Something a friend or colleague told you? Other?)

17. Among the companies you mentioned, which one, besides us, would you consider to be the best choice if you were making this decision now? What are this company's key strengths? What are this company's weaknesses? Are there changes about our company that we should make in order to be clearly superior to this competitor?

18. Do you anticipate buying more, or less, or about the same amount of <u>our product</u> next year? (If the customer answers "less", ask this follow-up

question. "Mr. Buyer, is there something else that you will buy in its place?

19. Do you regularly attend trade shows? If so, which ones do you think are relevant and informative?

20. Which professional and trade associations are you a member of that are specific to your line of business?

21. Do you shop online for (our product)? What search strategy do you use?

22. Are there newsletters and "e-zines" that you read regularly?

23. What other sources of information do you consider credible that help you make purchase decisions?

24. Please tell me a few basic facts about your company, if these facts are available from web site, ask to confirm its accuracy.

25. Length of time in business? - Size of company ($ revenue, # employees)?

26. Who (in addition to yourself) makes or influences purchasing decisions within your organization? What are the functional titles of decision-maker and influencers?

27. Ask the buyer to state this question with his own request: "If your firm would do BLANK for me, life would be so much easier?" After he states his wish, ask him to tell you all about BLANK and how he would find it useful.

28. What expectations do you have for me in returning your phone calls?

29. What was your thought process leading up to your purchase decision? How long did it take?

30. Did outside advisors (e.g., consultants, investors) play a role in your decision process?

31. Has our product/service enhanced your profitability? If so how?

32. May we use what you just told me as your "testimonial" about our product/service and its value to you on our website and brochures? (Be careful to get permission to use their name.)

33. Have you ever thought, "If only a company like ours could do (BLANK) mails, etc.? How quickly would you expect me to respond?

34. What is important to you about making a change at this time? Have you considered or tried to make a change in the past? What stopped you from considering a new (solution) last time?

35. What is your company's annual sales volume?

36. What is your expected outcome for our meeting today? What do you want to happen before we adjourn?

12 Steps To Locate New Customers Using Current Customers' SIC Codes From Your Free Library Card

Once you have a couple of customers you have sold to, you now can use their SIC code to find more similar companies in the same SIC category using a free library card, all online. Here are the steps

1. **Card:** Get yourself or your office a free local library card.

2. **Go Online**: Logon to your library website (city or county, i.e. Houstonpubliclibrary.org).

3. **Choose Research:** Go to the Research section of the website.

4. **Select Program:** Search for Reference USA – Remote User (one example of many options for company profiles or company mandatory reporting data).

5. **Select one known company**: You will have options to search information about one company or a complete group of similar potential customers. At this point, choose to select a known company and enter their name and address.

6. **Find firm's SIC code**: On the information that will be displayed will be the company's declared SIC code (Standard Industrial Code). If the firm is large and has lots of products or services, the firm may have several SIC codes. Select the first one which is supposed to be the dominant SIC choice and area of interest.

7. **Search for other firms with SIC code**:   You have the option to enter one or more SIC codes for the United States and get hundreds or thousands of other firms that have declared that SIC code as their own also (similar industry).

8. **Research report with multiple company names:** You will get a multi-page report with names, addresses, phone numbers and other corporate data to tell you how to contact these new potential customers.

9. **Sort selection options**:   You will have choices to sort companies by SIC code, groups of SIC codes, territorial areas or specific states, targets within certain mileage ranges and those over a sales size minimum. You will also find corporate organization charts for larger multi-branch firms that indicate the name and complete addresses of all of the subsidiaries and divisions of that selected company along with their respective sales totals.

10. **Search new company SIC Codes**: As soon as your company takes an order from a new company, assign someone in sales to research that new firm, find all of its sister divisions and locations on this same Reference USA (remote user version).

11. **Find new company branches**:   Have the person who researched the firm forward company literature to those branches building upon the initial sales order just received.

12. **Lure sister divisions in with price savings:**   Offer a corporate discount to all of those related sister

divisions since those sister divisions are now included.

32 Examples Of Answers From "I Wish…" Cards You Offer To Your Customers

Give your customers cards which contain the words, "I wish …." and ask if they will fill it out with something they would like to see changed or added or moved or stopped or started about your store. These answers may provoke great ideas for you and your management team. Here are examples of cards containing obvious great sales and marketing ideas that you might get back.

1. I wish your bakery **sold cinnamon buns**.

2. I wish your office hours started at **7:30 a.m. versus 8:00 a.**m. Traffic is high at 7:30 a.m. and subsides within 15 minutes of that.

3. I wish your produce department had **smaller portions** of some of the fruits and vegetables. I cannot eat the large portions being packaged and sold. They go bad at home. That's I why I don't buy strawberries because they sell too many at one time. I want a smaller container.

4. I wish you had the **"13 for a dozen" special** like your bakery competitor across town offers on Saturdays. They are always busy on weekends.

5. I wish your machine shop **offered 24/7 service**. Many shops need parts made on weekends and would pay a higher price if any shops were open then.

6. I wish your auto **mechanic business could come at night to my house,** pick up my vehicle, make the repairs and then bring it back before I have to leave

for work. If you did that, I would call you guys all of the time for all three of my cars.

7. I wish your bank branch had more parking. When it is crowded, I do not park there.

8. I wish you had **off brand cleaning supplies** like your competitor across the street.

9. I wish you had some **suggestions for recipes** for some of that foreign produce you sell. It looks good but I don't know what to do with it.

10. I wish your **clothes were sorted by size.** I get tired of looking for my size and just quit and go home.

11. I wish your store had **more lights in the front towards the parking lot**. I am afraid of those people asking for money in the parking lot every weekend.

12. I wish your personnel in the check cashing department **would text on their phones when there was fewer customers**. I wish your guards would help elderly people to their cars, especially after dark. I asked, but was told they are not allowed to escort anyone. I wish you had longer hours during the week; I cannot get here through the traffic before you close. (Review store revenue by time periods and consider changing or extending store hours, especially if this comment occurs frequently or your competitors close earlier than you.)

13. **I wish your website wasn't so confusing**. I tried to buy something once stopped; it did not seem very

safe using my credit card. The main problem is that it is hard to understand what to do next. Your instructions are too vague, the buttons to click are too small, (why white buttons on a white background?) and when I do click something, nothing happens so I leave the website. It hangs up too often and the email box you provide does not work. I hope you are not paying a lot to someone to manage that site; if you are, you are being cheated.

14. I wish it was **easier to return defective products in your store**. I do not know why it takes so long; you are understaffed and the ones that do work there have no authority; they must call a manager from the back of the store every time. Who set up this process? It is not working.

15. I wish your **sale items were more clearly marked**. More than once when I take items to the counter, they charge me the wrong price. (Who is responsible for marking products? Check and review the job description and discuss the task with the employee. Bad prices ruin customer loyalty and embarrass buyers who have to call out your employees' errors.)

16. I wish you would **mark 'sale items' with the right prices**. I have to argue with the clerk at checkout to get the right price because they are not marked, so when this happens, everyone is held up in line. I hate to buy anything when you have to deal with this unnecessary hassle.

17. I wish you had the **new fall pullover sweaters** in the front of the store offered in at least a couple of shades of red. Did you talk to anyone about the new colors that are out this year? (Who is the buyer? Can other shades be purchased quickly? if this was comment was received several times?)

18. I wish you had an **easier bag to carry**; this stiff paper handles cut into the carrier's hands. Your competitor has a really easy to carry bag with plastic on the handle; they just started using them about a month ago. (Ask marketing people to review packaging and the distributor for packaging options in the market.)

19. I wish your store was **not so cold** with the air conditioning; the air blows directly down on you when standing in line to check out. I know it is a little thing, but three people plus the clerk checking me out said the same thing. (See if an air deflector can be installed to divert air flow.)

20. I wish you had a **security guard in the parking lot** since there are no outside lights. I do not feel really safe outside after dark. (Who can be assigned after dark to make trips out to the lot or to escort shoppers from the front of the store?)

21. I wish it was easier to get hold of someone **when I call the store**. No one picks up even after I get a recorded message and try to hit "0". (What is the procedure and who is assigned in the front office to handle incoming calls? When that person is not working, who is the alternative?)

22. I wish you had an **extra person in the shoe department**. The man back there tries his best, but five or six people are waiting on one person and then you have personnel standing in other departments talking.

23. I wish someone would respond when **I send email inquiries on your website**. Sometimes I get a response but it is only a computerized general answer and does not answer my question. It is not worth trying to email anything when you cannot reach anyone.

24. I wish I could get some **help in your billings department** to get my account straightened out. One time my check cleared the bank and I showed this to your manager, but no one credited my account. The next time I came to the store, the manager changed and I had to start the process over.

25. I wish I could **push a buzzer in the aisle** or department to call for help (an employee or clerk) to help me when I have a question about a product. I cannot find anyone, and then by the time I get to the front of the store, I just go ahead and leave because it is useless to try to get anyone's attention.

26. I wish it was as **easy to get out of your store** as it is getting into your store. I hate to come in and find anything I want to buy because it is a hassle to pay for it.

27. I wish someone would **offer to help**; I look at your employees and they ignore me.

28. I wish I could look up products on a **simple keyboard at the front of your store** when I enter; something really simple where I enter four or five characters and it looks up the matching words and tells me the aisles or locations in the store, maybe with a simple map from where I am standing. It takes forever to find anybody and they normally say they don't know the part of the store that I ask about.

29. I wish you guys would **smile occasionally**. Too many people look depressed. I sometimes wonder about my safety in your store given the type of employees you have hired. They act bothered when I ask a question.

30. I wish there was an **easy way to get product instructions after I get home.** My problem is that I cannot find how to, 1. put my product together, 2. wash the piece of clothing I bought, 3. where to buy replacement parts, bulbs, fixtures, etc., 4. how to contact a repairman for this product, 5. how to contact the manufacturer. Is there an 800 number for these types of questions?

31. I wish your people were more **friendly when they answer the telephone**. They talk so fast, I cannot understand what they are saying. If they are busy, they cut me off or put me on hold. Am I the only one who has problems with getting through to someone in your organization? One day when the young lady cut me off, I simply called your competitor to place the $50,000 order. I did not know if you wanted to know that or not. I don't

even like to deal with your competition, but in a way, you forced me to call them, didn't you?

32. I wish I could ask someone there for a **history of what I have purchased over the last 12 months**. I bought some things but do not know their names. I wanted to buy some more but do not know the names of the articles. I wish I could see my purchases in chronological order. I asked someone this question once but they were certain this was impossible and if you did this for one, you would have to do it for everyone. I do not think that person is with you anymore.

13 Questions To Ask Customers Why They Chose You And 9 Actions To Keep Them

You need to know why customers choose your facility so you can take advantage of it throughout your company. Ask customers why they chose your store every day and compare the results. Here are some example questions you can choose from.

1. Ask all new customers starting today what caused them to call your company for a quote. You need to know because you spend a lot on finding and winning new customers and you must find out if your methods pay off or not.

2. Was the customer called upon by one of our sales personnel? If so, who and how well did the meeting go? Were all questions answered and follow-up comments resolved?

3. Did the customer initially read our website? If he did, was everything covered and explained well enough for him to make a decision?

4. Did the customer receive one of our brochures or advertisements in the mail? What about the mailer caught his eye or made him call our company?

5. Did the customer receive a referral from another company which suggested to try our company? If so, what company gave out our name? Has someone on our staff called that business to thank them for the referral?

6. Did the customer see our commercials or advertisements and then decide from those television spots to call us?

7. Did the customer notice our company's sponsorships of nonprofit organizations and that is what caused them to call for product quotes?

8. Did the customer see news stories mentioning our company's capabilities?

9. Did the customer happen to see the company trade show booth at the industry trade show? Did they talk to anyone who manned the booth and took questions?

10. Did the customer see our billboards?

11. Did the customer see our company vehicles with signs and phone numbers on all of the doors?

12. Did the customer drive past the plant and notice our displays in the yard?

13. Did the customer call us because of one of our employees (other than sales personnel)?

Actions to take for newly acquired customers:

1. In your database, keep track of why each customer came to your company initially. (i.e. mailer, referral, sales call, advertisement or some other notable reason)

2. Write the declared SIC code and SIC name for all new companies in your database to be extracted, sorted and used later (library sources are free of charge and accessible online).

3. Run all of the customers and sort them by their SIC code and then next by the type of effective advertising that worked.

4. Sort for the most frequent methods of advertising that seemed to work (i.e. 41% mailers, 28% physical sales calls, 18% telephone calls (solicitations))

5. Increase your efforts on the successful ideas and approaches. Do more advertising that brought in the most customers. Those obviously work better than all of the other methods for your particular business so use them to increase sales.

6. If the more effective rate is physical sales calls, hire more sales people.

7. If the more effective method for your firm is advertising in the local paper, buy a long term package deal and ask them to place it strategically within the weekly issues to boost your business.

8. If the more effective method for your company to get sales is cold calls, hire more outside sales people.

9. For the highest SIC code ranking, buy a list of companies that compete in that SIC code and aim a marketing campaign within that SIC code since your firm is already familiar with company types. You have the experience to deal with those firms so buy more names in the same industry.

21 Questions To Ask Your Sales Personnel In Order To Increase Sales

Questions you may want to ask when reviewing salesmens' sales reports.

1. What are the highest sales customers for this salesman?

2. Ask why those customers chose our company versus the competitors.

3. Ask which potential customers did not choose our company and the reasons that were stated by the buyer when he told the salesman that our company lost the bid.

4. Ask what we need to do in order to win more sales in the market.

5. Ask the sales representative what he is missing in order to get more sales?

6. Ask which customers are considering coming to our company and what can we do to entice them?

7. Is there just one large customer with 80% of the sales and just a few small ones?

8. What is the average dollar value of the sales order?

9. If there is a very large single order for the month, eliminate it and calculate the average sales order value for the rest of the orders which is a more reasonable ongoing dollar figure.

10. Are sales for this representative concentrated where he is located or is there a disconnection between his sales and his physical territory?

11. For the sales level this gentleman brings to the company, what are his sales expenses?

12. Does he spend more or less than his counterparts? (i.e. larger territory, more gas used, largest account in the company which costs more in lunch expenses, etc.)

13. Are the dollars he spends going to pay off? (Is your company getting orders from these potential customers yet?)

14. Are there new customers being added on a regular basis or one or two every six months?

15. Are there a number of assigned customers on the list that have yet to issue a purchase order to your company? Are there understandable reasons for this?

16. Ask the sales representative to tell you what he needs to increase sales.

17. Ask the laggard sales representative frequently who or what is holding him back from getting more sales. What else can the company do for him to help him secure more orders? You must eliminate all reasons that hinder getting new sales orders for the sales rep so you know if he needs training or replacement.

18. Make this sales report accessible at any given time to this sales representative. If necessary, assign an

inside person to run these reports for sales personnel as they call in. Also make sure the report is updated, all orders are entered quickly and completely into your system.

19. Are there any delays in entering new customer sales orders into your sales system? Ask the sales representatives to mention these missing dollars if they notice there are missing sales orders from their reports. Solve this problem quickly when you have salesman depending upon commissions and cannot see if they have generated any earnings. If they have to worry about this process, you have internal problems.

20. Ask the representative what else he needs to be added to the report? What would help him? Would a market estimate of new customers help him size up new potential sales?

21. Make sure all of the representatives have plenty of company literature and samples. Be concerned when these items are not being requested on a normal basis.

10 Roadblocks Your Sales Personnel Hit Every Day Inside Your Own Company

Employees in your own company sometimes create problems for your sales representatives who are trying to secure new business for the company. Employees many times do not know they may be the problem and not the solution. Review these examples of roadblocks your salespeople hit every day.

1. Your salesperson brings in a sample and purchasing tells them they cannot find the material defined in the specification. It is rare, difficult to find or maybe your people are inexperienced and embarrassed to ask.

2. Your salesperson asks if your firm can arrange international shipment and your freight manager says your company ships only domestically.

3. Your salesperson requests a product to be made in a specific color but your inexperienced engineers claim they cannot match the shade of blue requested AND they do not offer to call someone outside of the company.

4. Your salesperson indicates no one is reading the lengthy 49-page small print, no picture sales literature prepared only a couple of years ago and is quickly told there are too many copies left to throw away.

5. Your salespeople have brought RFQs (requests for quotes), but because your quoting process is too slow, most customers who initially asked, decided not to wait and chose other bidders long ago.

6. Your salespeople complain about the incentive programs because of the length of delay between getting an order and getting paid.

7. Your salespeople cannot get orders because they have many clerical tasks to finish inside the office minimizing face time with customers.

8. Your salespeople resist taking a drop in their base pay because they doubt they will be able to make the incentives in your company to replace the lost wages.

9. Your plant ships on time but has a reputation for rejects and returns ruining the bonus program for the salespeople.

10. When you ask your sales people what percentage of time they are talking to customers, they tell you less than 50% due to assigned tasks easily handled by a clerk inside.

10 Benefits Of Getting A Quote From Your Company

A very critical thing that the salesman must do is be able to give a quote to a customer. It is the only way to get their attention that they may be paying too much and your firm deserves another look. Here are reasons to tell the customer why he should get a quote from your firm.

1. Tell the buyer if your quote is relatively close, the company will be assured that they are currently getting a very competitive price in the market.

2. The buyer can take a lower bid and ask the current vendor to try to match or at least give in on the price difference. The worst that happens is the vendor declines. Once that occurs, the customer then may be able to negotiate other items in dispute since the vendor will feel compelled to say 'yes' at some point.

3. The buyer decides to accept your company's quote and then goes on to save money, something the buyer reminds his boss about at raise time.

4. Your firm states in the bid language there are no additional fees involved except those initiated by the buyer. The buyer who has been charged extra fees consistently by the old vendor now becomes more intelligent about the marketplace, starts to ask questions and will most likely be apt to consider your firm in the future if not now.

5. Your firm shrewdly submits two costs. You present one cost with the stipulated materials per the customer's specifications. You then qualify your

next bid which is substantially cheaper substituting other less costly materials. This will cause the buyer and his engineering team to discuss these potential cost savings and question their approach. Your action potentially provokes redesign and a material bottom line enhancement because you displayed options for your potential customer. Even if the option is denied, your firm now is regarded as sharp, aggressive and a positive influence on its customers.

6. Your firm gives pricing for the product produced or service provided with and also without freight (customer pickup). The buyer's current vendor charges a delivered charge and does not disclose the freight cost. If not considered by the buyer in the past, it will be now if the cost savings are substantial.

7. Your firm gives a bid for the item exactly as shown on the blueprints provided and then another much lower cost for a product redesigned with costs taken out by your seasoned cost engineers who do this every day.

8. Your firm shows the cost of the product with the buyer's supplied material and the lower cost of the product with material your firm buys in volume coupled with volume discounts. He's impressed and now a bit angry since his current vendor never offered this.

9. Your firm presents a bid on a grid with multiple selections including a price for quantity of 100, 500

and 1000. The grid offers pricing with and without freight at each level as well as pricing with and without material at each of the levels you choose. The buyer now sees cost reduction potential and if nothing else demands it from his current vendor. You establish yourself through this bid of an excellent alternative vendor in the future.

10. Your firm presents a bid and gives a price for all of the volume or 1/3 or ½ of the volume. When asked by the customer why the delineation, you indicate the customer should have alternative vendors which will keep the other in line. To get part of his work, indicate if he splits his current work among competing bidders, he will most likely get better service from both. Add, that competition is healthy for all parties.

25 Questions To Ask Your Sales Personnel

Take the time to talk to your sales personnel to find out what the market wants and what it does not want. Here is a list of questions you might ask of your sales personnel to find out your problems.

1. What is the easiest product/service of our company to sell?

2. What is the hardest product or service of our company to sell? And why are those products hard to sell?

3. What does the average American think about our company products?

4. Do they like them? If they like them but do not buy them, is that because they are getting what they need with cheaper alternatives?

5. Which products do the customers like the best?

6. Which of our products do the customers disregard as too pricey? Or unnecessary?

7. Which products do they think are too expensive or pricey?

8. Is our freight policy driving people away?

9. What are their reasons for not buying to buy our product?

10. What product is not popular, no matter what we do?

11. What product sells itself?

12. What are the best incentive programs we run for customers? Which were worthless and nonproductive?

13. What is the one attribute you tell potential customers about our company that surprises them?

14. What are we missing in our advertising campaign that would help sell the company?

15. What product or service does our company do a lousy job or making or performing?

16. Are there any services we should not offer to customers?

17. Are there any services we should offer to customers (that they request frequently)?

18. What are we missing from our product list we need to add in the future?

19. How would you change our advertising brochures to make it easier to sell?

20. What does the customer not seem to understand about our company? About our products/services?

21. What do people (buyers) want regardless of the price charged?

22. What product seems to have very little drop in demand regardless of how expensive it is?

23. Does it make any difference that we are only 47 miles from the shipping channel? 10 miles from the train station? 15 miles from a bus station?

24. Do we have enough inside sales staff? Do customers complain about how difficult it is to place an order?

25. Is there any inside sales person we have that we should consider replacing? Or offer further training?

20 Questions To Ask, Probe And Uncover About Your Competitors

Someone in your company must be assigned to researching the competition. Make sure this person will do the research necessary to understand how your firm should bid against these companies. These competitors have strengths but they also have their weaknesses. Find out both. Ask some or all of these questions about each to get started bidding more effectively.

1. **Size:** How big are they? What are their sales dollars $?

2. **Locations:** Where do they do business? You want to know this because you need to use their small size or concentration of only a few customers against them in bids.

3. **Age:** How long have they been around? If you have been around for fifty years and they started five years ago, you need to stress longevity and stability. You know what you are doing or you would have not have made it. The jury is out on your competitor. This leaves a lingering question in the mind of the buyer who must decide between you and the other guy.

4. **Coverage:** How much insurance do they have? Is it comparable? Why do they have less? Is it because they are not insurable? Have they had too many accidents and cannot obtain more insurance?

5. **Experience:** What jobs have they done and what customer do they have? Find out if they have had any problems. Do they really only serve one or two

major customers? Is it that difficult to find out what they have actually done?

6. **Employee turnover:** Does this competitor have a high employee turnover? You might watch incoming resumes and look for people who have worked there to find out information. Watch the job boards and see the ratings given by ex-employees. It is very important that you know what a company is like in order to compete with them. It is you against them.

7. **Legal problems:** Do they have problems paying taxes or filing documents with the state? Are they in good status or on hold? Check with your state attorney's office and see if they are in trouble. If they are, your salesmen need to know this.

8. **Vendor problems:** Do they have problems paying vendors? Ask your vendors if they have troubles getting paid by this competitor. Some vendors will tell you privately, some will not. This is the main reason you should always maintain an honest and solid relationship with all of your vendors. Try to treat them as well as your employees and they will always help you. They can be your best friends in the world or they can crucify you in the market when you do not pay them. You make the decision.

9. **Win ratio or history:** What jobs have they won lately? What type of work do they do best?

10. **Competitive advantages:** What types of products do they offer that no one else offers? What projects do they avoid?

11. **Can they be bought?** If they are really attractive and all the factors are favorable, is this competitor for sale?

12. **Who are the owners?** Find out if this is a private firm, foreign owned or held by a trust or people behind a management group.

13. **Unionized?** Does the firm have good employee relations or do they suffer from frequent strikes?

14. **Publicly or privately held?** Public companies are much easier to evaluate though you must consider that private firms must be doing something right after thirty years. If they were not, negative cash flow would have steered them off the road a long time ago.

15. **D&B rating?** Credit worthiness?

16. **Delivery** time acceptable?

17. **Customer service** good?

18. **Reputation** well know or newcomer?

19. **Any competitive bids** in the past? Have we won against this competitor in prior bids? Do they lowball? Do they have reasonable pricing? Do any of our salespeople know outside customers who have done business with this competitor? What are their feelings or thoughts?

20. **Multiple competitors** or just a limited few? This makes a difference so have your sales people list every competitor that is out in the active market. They may not all be one to one comparisons since all firms have differing capabilities. Physically line

up those close to you in order to start some comparisons.

Know your competitors and offer what they do not.
When you think you have discovered everything there is to know about all of your competitors, no company should be driven by a strategy that is based on beating the competition. The best strategy to follow is doing what customers want and doing it well.

Spend your money to study customers, not competitors.
It is good to know the competition, but your best spent money is invested in studying your customers and constantly improving your products and services. If you make them happy, they will not look really hard for your competitors.

8 Questions To Ask Your Shipping Personnel About How They Treat Customers' Truck Drivers

1. What do you think these truck drivers see when they are standing around waiting to be loaded here in our dock?

2. Does anyone make sure they are aware of the restrooms and a place to get water or access to a telephone (if they ask)?

3. Do you or someone in the shipping department go up to them and ask what they need, or out of courtesy, politely inform them how long it will be if the department is busy?

4. Are accommodations made for these special drivers? If possible, your people should give these people preferential treatment and push their product out the door first before other 3rd party freight companies (i.e. DHL, FedEx, and Saia).

5. Is everyone in the shipping department nice to them without exception? Make sure they are. You do not need negative stories taken back and repeated multiple times among their company buyers.

6. Does anyone ask them questions or speak to them? Do you ask if this is there first or last stop? Where else they are going? How long they have worked for the customer or if they are busy or not? They may not want to talk or they might. You will not know unless you try to be friendly. Show an

interest in their comfort and go out of the way to help them if they have a problem.

7. Do those customers' drivers observe any bad behavior from your department personnel? How do you know and what makes you think that everything is perfect in the shipping department after hours?

8. Did you ask if there was anything wrong with coming to our facility? Did you ask if they had problems getting into the plant, any problems backing in or is there anything we can do to make loading up easier and faster for them?

When training your people in shipping, tell them they must assume that those drivers are questioned about what goes on at the vendor's facility. Your people must make sure that only good information is conveyed to the customers' buyers if anything is said. You cannot assume that it is not important.

24 Questions To Ask Your Company Drivers To Cut Waste, Improve Service And Reduce Delivery Cost

Questions for freight delivery personnel about waste, cutting costs, customer feedback and general observations:

1. Are there any trips you are making now as a driver that are wasteful and could possibly be eliminated?

2. Are you making any repeated trip each week where cutting the number from four or five down to two or three trips would suffice? Give a specific example.

3. Is there a better way to buy fuel at a cheaper rate? Must the products be sent on our truck? Can they be mailed normal carrier?

4. Are you given everything you need before you leave to make deliveries?

5. Are the instructions provided for your trips to get to the customers' facilities adequate or do they result in you being late, directed to wrong addresses or otherwise incomplete or incorrect too often?

6. What do you suggest should be changed or modified or added or subtracted from the drivers' instructions provided to you prior to your departure that would expedite and help you on your trips?

7. Are we wasting money on our trucks? What do we need to change or alter? (i.e. gas put in other non-authorized vehicles, gas card abuse, no control on spending on company credit cards, no oversight on driving records, excess accidents, people take

vehicles home, people use company cars and trucks for personal use, vehicles not maintained as required, too much damage unreported, drive off accidents or damage)

8. Do you see any cost savings that we are missing concerning freight costs?

9. Are our trucks outdated? Lousy on gas mileage? Do they break down too often?

10. Do we need to consider buying a new truck or truck(s)?

11. Do you think we have too many drivers? What makes you say this?

12. If you had to reduce trips down per week, where would you do it?

13. Are there trips we are making where you think we lose money? (i.e. Long delayed waits, damaged shipments, false claims by customer employees).

14. Of all of the facilities that you visit, which stops are the worst? Why are they the worst?

15. Of all of the customers' facilities where you make deliveries, which do you not trust? If there are none, which do you regret visiting and why?

16. Which of the customers' facilities take the most time to deliver?

17. Do you ever see any questionable activities within our own organization when you are picking up or dropping loads?

18. Do you ever see any concerning or questionable activities when you are picking up or dropping off at the customers' facilities?

19. Are there any problems with pulling in, loading and exiting our company facility and loading dock? Is it easy, difficult, taking time to maneuver or cause problems and delays because of the design or flaws with the way the dock is currently built?

20. If you could change the company dock(s) in any way, what would it be?

21. What is the worst problem for unloading and loading at the outside customers' facilities? Is there any equipment you need that would speed up the process or make it easier and safer?

22. Which customer has the worst facility for truck access and unloading in your opinion? Why do you say this specifically concerning the layout of the unloading facility?

23. Which customer facility takes the longest time to unload, get paperwork signed and dated and then ultimately get approval and clearance to leave?

24. Which facility is the best to unload? Why?

22 Questions To Ask The Truck Drivers Who See And Speak To Your Customers Every Day

Talk to the guys who speak to your customers every day. They are the same ones who see your competition pull up to the customer's dock also. Speak to the truck drivers who speak to your customers every day. Talk to him. Ask him some questions and thank him for the good insight he will give you. Here are a few questions to consider.

1. Ask what is done with your product once it reaches the customer's site?

2. Do our products sit on the dock for long?

3. Are our products taken to racks or handled by overhead cranes? Any problems?

4. Are our products visually inspected?

5. Are our products dropped or abused in any way that the buyer might not know about?

6. Ask if the product is unwrapped or taken off the pallet or changed in any way once it is delivered.

7. Ask if the customer's quality control department comes and tests the product right away?

8. Does the customer test count the items on the pallets that were sent?

9. Is the company driver held up for any reason before signing off on the packing lists?

10. Does the customer just sign the paperwork without checking the contents or any of the pallets or boxes?

11. Do the customer's QC inspectors come to check the delivered load?

12. Does the customer physically open the boxes and test count any of the items shipped?

13. Does the customer have any problems opening our company's packaging, pallet-wrap, containers, etc.?

14. Does the customer make out a separate receiving ticket completely different from packing list that your firm sent with the goods?

15. You want to know if the expensive packaging you had designed is torn off and discarded once your product arrives at the customer's door. Are we over-packaging our product? This would tell you to completely relook at packaging that is currently overbought and unnecessary.

16. You want to know if testing occurs immediately or if this is most likely done at a later date. You want to know what the procedure is and if there is anything about your product that creates problems for handling by the customers' employees (a potential irritating problem that needs to be eliminated before they squawk too much to the buyer).

17. You want to know if your product poses any unnecessary problems for the customer. If the driver delivers to this customer frequently, ask him what other problems occur at the loading dock of this customer.

18. What are the main problems that other competing vendors have? We want to know the competition's weakness.

19. Is this customer' dock a difficult place to unload?

20. Does this customer seem organized or sloppy and unsupervised?

21. Did the customer ever comment about what is wrong with our company's products?

22. What else could our company do to improve the product, packaging, packing list information (what info is missing?)?

11 Questions To Ask Visitors About Your Website

1. **Unique information?** Does your website provide information not found anywhere else? If not, why waste one's time searching on your website for anything?

2. **Interesting useful search results?** Does your search engine provide different, unique and interesting results unlike your competitors? If not, you better be the cheapest since you add no value, plus you just wasted the visitor's time.

3. **Learning experience?** Do your visitors feel they have learned something once they visit your website? If they do not, you are either selling a commodity and everything is driven by price or, you are about to slowly go out of business, unless you are a nonprofit.

4. **Representative website?** Does one get the sense that your business is well represented by the pictures and content provided on the website? If not, what is the reason you are hiding your firm and what is it that you actually sell?

5. **Difficult query?** Does a visitor have to click numerous times just to get to an answer, or is the answer to his question easy to find? Be warned; visitors will not search for long, and if they do, they will not be back.

6. **Updated and thorough database?** Do you retain all searches in order to ultimately update the

database of your search engine? If you must ask why, you need to seek outside help in managing your website since you are ignoring your potential market.

7. **Deserving of 'favorite' status?** Do you give the visitor a reason to mark your website a 'favorite'? If you do not, why not? Is there any reason to come back to your website for anything?

8. **Easy-to-find telephone number?** Does the visitor have difficulty finding your toll-free or local telephone number or does it appear on every page? Is it easy to find with a quick glance?

9. **Missing key data of a real business?** Does your website look suspect because it's lacking a physical address, or telephone number or email address? Do you not want visitors and potential customers to contact you?

10. **Limited search results?** Do you frustrate visitors who want to search but get few options from your search option? If you are sure to disappoint them, be assured you will not have to worry about appeasing them the next time, since they will not be back.

11. **Is it easy to contact your company?** Providing no telephone number and only an email option means you do not want to talk to potential customers. Did you actually wonder to yourself why you get so few inquiries, given the barriers you have created? Would you respond well to a website you visited that makes it difficult to speak with someone?

34 Questions To Ask Everyone In Order To Improve Your Website

When developing your website, do not neglect to ask visitors (employees, customers, vendors and others) questions about the site and their experience. You want to know if the site is or is not doing what you intended.

Here are some questions to consider asking in order to make on-going improvements to that website.

1. If you speak another language, would you like for the website to be offered in another language?

2. Would you like to see foreign words added to the search bar?

3. Did you like the company website? If you did not, please explain why.

4. Was it easy to find the toll-free telephone number? Did you call the number?

5. If you wanted to contact the company, was it easy to do so from the website? Does more information need to be posted in a conspicuous place on the screen?

6. Was there a call to action at nearly every screen change? Was it easy to know what to do next, step by step? If not, discuss which web page was confusing or loses the visitor? What can be improved or added?

7. Was it easy to navigate on the website? Was it easy to find what you wanted?

8. Did the data search work? Was the data search missing the terms you entered? What terms did you enter that came up missing or not found? Did you find what you were looking for? If not, what did you not find?

9. Did the website's search engine work well or poorly, compared to other similar websites?

10. What would you like to see about the search function on the company's website that could be improved?

11. Did you want to stay on the website or did you have an urge to leave?

12. Was the website boring? Interesting? What is missing in your opinion that can be improved?

13. Did the company website make you want to return or give up and leave?

14. Was it easy to find the items you wanted to buy, or to find the items in which you were interested?

15. Did you learn anything new about the company from the website? What did you learn?

16. What did you want to learn that you did not?

17. Is the information that you learned on the company website relevant to you as a potential customer? Did it make you change your mind about the company?

18. Was it easy enough to review the items thoroughly enough to buy them on the website? If not, what is the reason you would not buy them from this

company website? Are these items you would not buy on the internet, regardless of the website?

19. If you do buy these types of items from the internet, do you buy them often or is this the first time?

20. Did the website make it easy to decide to buy or purchase the items?

21. Did you call the toll-free 800 number for assistance? Was it easy to find the number to call for help or assistance?

22. Did you call the company for any assistance or talk to any inside sales personnel?

23. Was the website understandable and easy to follow?

24. Even if the website did not feature your native language, were there enough illustrations to allow you to understand what was being sold?

25. What about the website made you decide not to buy?

26. Did the website make you feel uncomfortable about buying any of the products?

27. Was there any time or point while on the website that you wondered what to do next because the site's instructions were not clear and did not seem to be intuitive?

28. If the instructions were not clear, was this the reason you did not buy?

29. If you did not buy, what was the reason?

30. Were you not looking for the product, but just browsing?

31. Were you not impressed with the product offerings? Why not?

32. Was there something about the products with which you were not pleased or you wish were different? Please describe what items need to be changed. Describe how they should be changed.

33. Was there any screen that was not clear concerning what to do next or what options were available to you? Which screen was the problem screen?

34. If you want to offer any comments or criticism, write your complaints or suggestions here. We will include you in our monthly suggestion contest (prepaid debit cards awarded for great ideas from our customers).

-My Checklist-

-My Checklist-

-My Checklist-

361

-My Checklist-

-My Checklist-

_____

_____

_____

_____

_____

_____

_____

_____

_____

_____

_____

_____

_____

_____

_____

_____

_____

_____

_____

_____

_____

_____

_____

-My Checklist-

-My Checklist-

-My Checklist-

Printed in Great Britain
by Amazon

84627956R00208